# PRACTICAL METAPHYSICS

# PRACTICAL METAPHYSICS

## A New Insight in Truth

ERIC BUTTERWORTH

Unity Village, Missouri

Practical Metaphysics
First Edition 2017

Compiled by: Mark Hicks
Edited by: Michael A. Maday

Cover design: Karen Rizzo
Interior design: *CreateSpace.com*

ISBN-13: 9780871593696
ISBN-10: 0871593696
Library of Congress Control Number: 2017955421
Unity Books
Canada BN 13252 0933 RT

**Also by Eric Butterworth**

*Spiritual Economics*
*Discover the Power Within You*
*In the Flow of Life*
*Unity: A Quest for Truth*
*Celebrate Yourself!*
*Breaking the Ten Commandments*

# TABLE OF CONTENTS

*"We need larger maps. We need a larger thought of God and a new insight of ourselves."*

—Eric Butterworth

# Acknowledgement

Eric Butterworth, the renowned Unity minister and teacher, was also a celebrated author. His books *Discover the Power Within You, Spiritual Economics,* and *Unity: A Quest for Truth* became national best-sellers. He also produced numerous popular audiocassettes based on his classes, and in 1981 provided us with "*A Course in Practical Metaphysics,*" in a two-volume set of tapes.

Mark Hicks, a licensed Unity teacher in Austin, Texas, and founder of *truthunity.net,* has for years been searching the Unity archives for treasures that people today would still value, bringing numerous works online. In 2016 he transcribed the Butterworth class recordings for a book he thought would serve those who might not have access to digital media. In 2017 that transcribed book drew the attention of Mary Earls, then vice president of communications at Unity, who recognized both the value of the work and its need for editing. Michael Maday, former editor of Unity Books, was then contracted to edit the book.

We want to acknowledge our debt to Mark Hicks for honoring our heritage and providing his loving service.

# FOREWORD
By Michael A. Maday

I T IS CURIOUS that Eric Butterworth, the finest teacher in the Unity spiritual movement and one of its best writers, did not actually write a book on practical metaphysics. He mentioned the topic from time to time to explain what Unity is, usually using the phrase "a new insight in Truth," which is an intriguing way of introducing it. He did teach classes on the subject and produced a cassette album in 1981 called *A Course in Practical Metaphysics*. The content of that class was made available online and turned into transcripts by Mark Hicks, the founder of *truthunity.net*, and then into something resembling Eric's prose by yours truly. That is the book you hold in your hands.

I often thought, as I worked on every page, removing the informal side comments that a class would enjoy but that might distract a reader, or bringing the paragraphs together in a more linear way to support understanding, how much I wished Eric himself had *written* the thing. Anyone who has ever dealt with written transcriptions of a talk knows the difference between that and actual prose, and Butterworth's prose was often sublime.

Eric Butterworth has been one of the biggest influences on my ministerial career. His books have all been seminal and he has modeled for me, and for many, how to be a Unity minister. His work as a radio broadcast pioneer, through his widely popular *Eric Butterworth Speaks*, rivaled his Sunday talks at Avery Fisher Hall in New York City as the most effective means of teaching practical metaphysics. My latest connection with his teachings came through Rev. Tom Thorpe, a talented and erudite Unity minister and teacher, who offered a wonderfully playful and profound series on Unity Online Radio called *Discovering Eric Butterworth*, which I was fortunate enough to support as his cohost for a year and a half. Butterworth's wisdom flowed through us, and it was a delight.

The word *metaphysical* seems strange to some. If we go back to the ancient Greeks, especially Aristotle, we find this idea that truth is derived from the study of natural processes (*physike*). *Metaphysics* literally means "beyond the science of nature." Academically, metaphysics is the branch of philosophy that studies the ultimate reality (Truth) beyond the physical realm and generally asks these perennial questions: What is the nature of being? What is the nature of the universe? How do we know what we know? Unity metaphysics also asks: What is the nature of God and humankind? What is the relationship between God and humankind? God is known as Spirit, the invisible life and intelligence underlying all physical things. And as the intelligence underlying all things, God is often referred to as Divine Mind. According to the Unity dictionary, *The Revealing Word* (p. 132), *metaphysics* is defined as "the systematic study of the science of being; that which transcends the physical."

Also starting with Unity cofounder Charles Fillmore, however, is a tradition of reserving the right to change our minds. In *Jesus Christ Heals* (p. 126) he wrote, "We are receiving new Truth in all fields, and if we are to use it, it seems most important that our religion be progressive, that we get new and higher concepts, and that we see deeper and more scientific relationships in the lessons and experiences of those who have preceded us in study and demonstration of spiritual Truth." So here is a key element in Unity beliefs, that metaphysical Truth keeps an open door, that knowledge is a living thing, and knowledge increases as more light enters human consciousness.

Unity from its beginning in 1889 has been an eclectic movement, a uniquely American mix, a melting pot of beliefs. Unity believes ideas that were previously not allowed to be expressed, ideas that were considered heresy. Unity champions those beliefs, but today that freedom of belief and expression is often taken for granted. Sometimes it is said that Unity is a return to first-century Christianity, or a Christianity that was not yet truly formed. Back then, Jesus' followers were, of course, Jews and usually called themselves "the Way." Unity, too, in its early years called itself "the Unity Way." Yet the basic idea still survives that we want to learn the teachings of Jesus and apply them in our lives, and that application is crucial, and is why our metaphysical movement has often been called "practical Christianity." But to both founders, Myrtle and Charles Fillmore, it was through the lens of metaphysics that we see the most. Charles liked to say he believed in the teachings of Christianity if they were "spiritually discerned." That was looking beyond the literal meanings to find their deeper meanings. Butterworth himself said many times, our job is "not to set things right but to see them rightly."

E.E. Slosson long ago wrote these words in his *Sermons of a Chemist* that help explain this metaphysical lens, how it shifts the way we see our spirituality: "A symbol is like a pane of glass, something to be seen through, not to be looked at. When it gets old, dusty, and opaque, then it becomes the object instead of the medium. Successive generations come to the window through which their ancestors, or perhaps only a keen-eyed mystic, formerly saw the light of heaven. But in the course of centuries the glass has darkened and become obscured by neglect to keep it clean, or encrusted with the gold and gems with which the pious devotees have adorned it. Still many have come, knelt before the window, and gone away pretending that they, too, have seen the heavenly vision; and some go away sneering and, because they see nothing through the glass now, they say that nobody ever did, that the first man was a liar and the rest were hypocrites."

To learn practical metaphysics, we are involved in something truly original. We will learn principles and teachings, but nothing has come predigested, and at some point we realize, we need to do the digesting! We can question ideas, and some of our ideas will be discarded, others altered, some strengthened. And some totally new ideas will come our way. Practical metaphysics will change our minds and the direction of our lives. We can have a personal revelation of Truth without relying on anyone else's vision. This is practical spirituality, and we are expected to put into practice what we have learned. It is all meant to be lived 24/7 and there is no greater challenge in life than that.

So we need what I call our metaphysics to be practiced, to be *practicable* metaphysics. We need it to be a faith that we diligently practice every day, perhaps every minute, as the teaching "pray without ceasing" suggests. Herein Eric Butterworth makes his case for this too. He had a delicious metaphor for this need that I've always savored. He called it a "relentless stream of Truth," and in many ways this stream goes back to Plato and the archetypal forms that can easily be seen as divine ideas.

This underground stream resurfaced in America at the turn of the 19th century amid the Industrial Revolution that brought social and economic changes all over the world, accompanied by a corresponding spiritual awakening. Poets, writers, philosophers, and religious leaders all contributed to this stream. It came to be called New Thought, and it included Unity, Christian Science, Religious Science, and Divine Science, to name the bigger movements. Today they include Agape and the Centers for Spiritual Living. They were what Butterworth called the "new insight in Truth." And they have gone on to greatly influence what in more recent times have come to be known as the Human Potential, Holistic Health, and New Age movements, among others. They are the spiritual but not religious movements.

Many of us have become spiritual consumers as the marketplace has grown exponentially in the past decades, aided first by the influx of great teachers from the East, and then by technology that makes esoteric teachings available in seconds by a click on your electronic device. This is both a great boon and a challenge, even a danger. The boon is obvious but the challenge may not be, for it allows us to take too much for granted, to follow the wisdom of the old saying, "Easy come, easy go." We momentarily find but don't really appreciate, and then go on searching for the next thing, the newest teaching, the sexiest new thrill in our digitized spiritual marketplace.

Here Butterworth has wisdom to offer. As you read this book, you can gain appreciation for his efforts to clarify what this practice actually entails. To give one example, in the final chapter on "Demonstration," he takes pains to clarify that the "who" who demonstrates is not the personality/ego but rather the essence we already are, the Christ Self. The personality/ego must surrender to the divine essence within and then awaken to its wisdom. That surrender is what allows the demonstration to flow through us. We do not "demonstrate" so much as we allow the "imprisoned splendor" to escape, as the great poem "Paracelsus" by Robert Browning says so well.

Since the poem is a Butterworth staple and not otherwise quoted in the text, I am providing it here:

> "Truth is within ourselves; it takes no rise
> From outward things, whate'er you may believe.
> There is an inmost center in us all,
> Where truth abides in fullness; and around,
> Wall upon wall, the gross flesh hems it in,
> This perfect, clear perception—which is truth.
> A baffling and perverting carnal mesh
> Binds it, and makes all error; and to know
> Rather consists in opening out a way
> Whence the imprisoned splendor may escape,
> Than in effecting entry for a light
> Supposed to be without."

Practical metaphysics is about developing and supporting the business of fully expressing our God nature, each of us doing what Jesus suggested we do with our lives, following in his footsteps, knowing that all he did we can do too, and more. In the words of one of Eric Butterworth's favorites, Ralph Waldo Trine, in *In Tune With the Infinite*, "God is no respecter of persons. He doesn't create prophets, seers, sages, and saviors as such. He creates people. But here or there one recognizes his or her true identity, recognizes the oneness of life and the Source whence it came. This one now lives in the realization of this Oneness, and in turn becomes a prophet, seer, sage, or savior."

So we are all sages in the making, releasing the imprisoned splendor and letting the light shine, bringing the kingdom into our world.

*Rev. Michael A. Maday, M.A., was ordained a Unity minister in 1984 and has served churches in Michigan and Missouri as well as Unity Village, Missouri, where he has been book editor for Unity Books, adjunct faculty for Unity Institute® and Seminary, and prayer associate for Silent Unity®.*

# 1

## ALLNESS OF GOD

### METAPHYSICS IS NOT TO BE STUDIED BUT PRACTICED

THE GREEK PHILOSOPHER Zeno sets a tone that I always like when he says, "The most important part of learning is to unlearn our errors."

Most of us have had some background in religious teachings, and we've already gotten involved in having to unlearn a few things. It may be a result of much of our metaphysical studies, if you have had such background. There may also need to be some unlearning because metaphysics is not a thing in and of itself any more than religion is a thing. It's a kind of perception and, like all perceptions, we see them in many ways and at many different levels. I like calling it "a new insight in Truth."

Whenever you hear teachers talk about the various laws of metaphysics, they're using a great deal of liberty in giving teaching symbols. These are fine and helpful. Metaphysics is basically a way of seeing life, a way of seeing the universe, a way of seeing spiritual thought. All they can do is deal with abstractions in trying to help us see a little more clearly. We're using the term "practical metaphysics" and by this, we're not at all being judgmental and suggesting that there are certain metaphysical teachings that are impractical. This is not the implication at all. We simply want to make a strong point that it is all too common to substitute intellectuality for actual practice. One can become a student of religion in the sense that he or she is well-versed in the religious teachings learned in catechism and be able to express the various prayers, and know when to sit down and stand up in church. Metaphysics is not of that nature. We're dealing with something that is to be practiced, therefore it must be practical. Unfortunately, many of us enter into the study of metaphysics with the same intellectual fervor that we do when studying mathematics or studying various religious teachings—learning the codes, learning the creeds, learning the treatments and the affirmations, feeling that this is what it's all about.

This is not what it's all about. We're concerned, essentially, with life. We're concerned, as Emmet Fox used to say, with consciousness, with feelings, with attitudes. As Jesus said, "By their fruits, you shall know them." We're basically concerned with demonstrating the fruits of the metaphysical system in terms of healthy-mindedness, in terms of greater health of body, greater peace of mind, greater prosperity in our affairs, greater love in our relationships, greater peace in our world. This is the proof. We expect to have that kind of proof, and if it doesn't demonstrate itself, then forget the whole thing.

We have lived most of our lives at what the Irish poet William Butler Yeats calls the "whirling circumference" of life. We've lived out at the circumference, out in human experience. In metaphysical insight, we realize that there is a depth within us. There's something more involved in life, that you can't actually understand life by appearances at the circumference, that you can never really know who you are by looking at yourself in a mirror. There's always something more, something deeper, something richer, something finer.

## METAPHYSICS IS PHYSICAL AND REPEATABLE

The term *metaphysics* has normally been defined very simplistically as "beyond the physical." This would seem to be the literal interpretation, but it's not adequate. Perhaps the best connotation is not *beyond* the physical, but *between* levels of life. If we think of the study of that which is beyond, sometimes we tend to go too far beyond in centering our attention. Thus we begin to come up with the concept that certain metaphysical teachings have done, that the body and matter is unreal or doesn't really exist. We then tend to deal with abstruse abstractions that really make very little practical sense in terms of relating them to human experience.

We think that metaphysics is not beyond the physical at all but rather a perception of a higher dimension of the physical. Practical metaphysics is the persistent attempt to relate to the reality beyond appearances but as a dimension of that experience. In other words, we always keep the concept of the whole. We don't go so far that we will lose sight of the whole experience.

Metaphysical teachers make a special point of tracing metaphysics to antecedents of comparatively recent times. I was just thinking of the American version of metaphysics as beginning with Phineas Parkhurst Quimby or of Mary Baker Eddy or perhaps Charles Fillmore or the more contemporary Emmet Fox—all pioneers of the new insight in Truth. There's a tendency toward a great deal of chauvinism or personal cultism as to which brand or flavor of Truth is best. It's like looking out on the landscape where several different people are sitting. They say, "I see a tree. I see a hill. The tree looks this way and then the hill is shaped in this way," and perhaps even itemizing it, describing it on a little notepad. Then they sit with one another arguing as to which view is the real thing. This is it just because this is the way I see it.

All religious systems, all metaphysical systems, as we have said, are basically a perception, a way of seeing things. There's no such thing as a right or wrong way. The important thing is: It is an experience that I'm involved in right now and therefore, it's right for me. In tracing the antecedents of metaphysics, I like to at least go far enough back to where we can get away from the cultish thought. I like to trace it back to someone who has outwardly demonstrated the process as far as we understand it. I think of the great metaphysician as Jesus. Now, obviously, Jesus himself would likely say, "But it didn't start with me." He didn't create the laws. He didn't create the laws of mind action. He didn't create the consciousness of divine love. He discovered them as one of many who had discussed them. He himself said, so to speak, "Before Abraham was, I am, so don't look to me. Look to that which I am looking at."

Jesus taught the infinite potential of man and the influence of the Allness of God. He said, "What I have done, you can do." This is the missing link in Christian religion. "All that I have done, you can do, too." Any great demonstration of law is repeatable. We tend to spend too much time looking to the people who demonstrate the law rather than the act of demonstration itself. Whenever anything is done, it shows that it can be done. The principle is what God has done, God can do, and God can do for you because you are involved in the same infinite law.

Practical metaphysics deals with what I call a "repeatable Christ." This is a hard step for people who have been immersed in the Christian tradition. Jesus was certainly God, but if Jesus demonstrated the law, the law is demonstrable. Therefore, it can be done at any time by one who is in that consciousness. Jesus deals with a repeatable Christ, and that's what we're involved in—a constant creative process at being in the Christ Consciousness—that's present at every point in time and space in much the same way as Jesus himself saw it.

## What Religion Really Is

I'm sure a lot of us have grown up under the influence that religion is a thing. Maybe you were sent to church to study religion because your parents thought you should have "religion" as part of a good background. You learned religion like you learned to do mathematics. You dealt with all sorts of structural parts of this cosmology that were presented as religion—God in heaven above, earth and human life beneath, hell and Satan under the earth. All these were a part of the process that many of us have been exposed to. So now religion may have become something we have to unlearn before we can proceed further.

Too often we fail to really get it together, to integrate our religious training in terms of our life experience in the here and now. This is what religion should be in a classic sense. The word *religion* means "to bind together." Religion actually means "unity." It means "oneness" and "wholeness." It's not just God out there, not just some imminent part in the universe where something can happen, not just a shrine where great healings take place, but all things bound together. We're in it and of it all the time.

Unfortunately, religions have tended to present themselves as institutions instead of perceptions, something you join instead of a transcendence you experience. We've tended to believe that God works exclusively through the machinery of an institution, so it is self-evident that most people believe you go to church to get close to God. The fact is, if God is present in the church, God is also present in a theater and a casino. God is present, period. God is an omnipresence, everywhere present, so you don't go to church to get close to God. You go to church, perhaps, hopefully, to be challenged to dig within yourself and to find that consciousness of the Presence that is with you wherever you go; so that wherever you go, wherever you are, God is.

I like to occasionally remind myself of the vision of Paul's sermon on Mars Hill, which you will find in the 17th chapter of Acts. This is especially noteworthy because it's an integral part of the scriptures that is read and studied by most fundamentalist Christians. However, it tends to present a point that would seem to belie a lot of the attitudes that are current throughout these religious teachings. In fact, it is an eye-opening realization for all ministers and for anyone who goes to church to find God.

Let's just consider what this says: "The God who made the world and everyone and everything in it, being Lord of heaven and earth, does not live in shrines made by man." We should emphasize that. "God … does not live in shrines made by man, nor is he served by human hands as though he needed anything, since he gives to all men life and breath and everything. Yet, he is not far from each one of us, for in him, we live and move and have our being" (Acts 17:24-25, 28). That's a fundamental realization, something that would be well-advised to be read in all church services. However, I suspect that if it were, it would be given an interpretation that would alter its meaning. Otherwise, what point is there in going to church?

## GOD IS AN ALLNESS IN WHICH I EXIST AS AN EACHNESS

The greatest discovery of modern times is that although the life of humankind and the world is incomplete and imperfect—there is a perfect whole. This is true regardless of whether you can see it or feel it. We are forced by a hidden instinct to reunion with parts of the larger heart of the universe. In other words, this explains the instinctive urge to know God. From the beginning of time, there has been this compulsion, this urge, this hunger, this desire to find and relate to the transcendence. This is something that is found in primitive people, no matter where. There's always been this urge for transcendence.

You see, we tend to get very confused in terms of what this does to our senses and our feelings. The desire to find and know God quite often misleads us to look for a God or to look for something anthropomorphic, which is personal, a kind of super-human, which is out there somewhere at some time and space. You see, God is not a person "out there." That's shocking to a lot of people. God is a presence that is ever-present and all present or, to put it in its most complete sense, God is an Allness in which I exist and you exist as an eachness.

Don't take that too lightly. Let that run through your consciousness a little bit—*God is an Allness in which you exist as an eachness*. In other words, to use the term *expression*, "I am an expression of God." The word *express* means "to stand forth." I am the Allness or the activity of the love and the substance and the life of God, standing forth at this point, not just in me, not working through me, not surrounding me, not putting his hands upon me, not guiding me, not directing me. All this, and so much more standing forth *as* me. Make a great mental note of that word *as*. God expresses *as* me. Otherwise, we tend to go back into the anthropomorphic relationships of God guiding me, directing me. God has his hands on my shoulder. God has the whole world in his hands and all of these things—God's eyes, God's ears, God's mouth, God's feet—all these things, which you find in the anthropomorphisms that are expressed in the Old Testament of the Bible, tell us something about the need for evolution, which has found more fulfillment in the New Testament. You see, we need to somehow transcend all this and get the realization of God as an *Allness* in which I exist *as an eachness*.

The contemporary philosopher George Santayana says that God is a "floating literary symbol." I like that term. God is a three-letter word, G-O-D. Quite often, a person will say, "Oh, I love God." More often than not, people love an abstraction. She loves a word. She loves an image that is anthropomorphic, the Michelangelo-like image up on the ceiling of the Sistine Chapel, the long white-bearded creature sitting on a throne somewhere. The fact is, in most cases, when we say, "I love God," what we're really saying is, "I love G-O-D. I have faith in G-O-D. G-O-D walks beside me. G-O-D guides me." We're talking about this floating literary symbol, this intellectualization of something that has no real relative sense in our life.

There was a time in the British Empire when they were having great troubles throughout their far-flung empire around the world, and the navies that were involved in taking care of its defense. One of the admirals sitting in the admiralty in Britain said to one of the royal heads, "Sir, I think we need larger maps." The fact is, if we're going to understand ourselves in modern times and relate religion and spiritual things to human experience, we need larger maps. We need a larger thought of God and a new insight of ourselves. Our God is not great enough. This is why so many people were upset and concerned during the first years of the U.S. space program. They were concerned that maybe we would find the domain of God out there on the other side of the moon.

The fact is: God is not to be found. God is nowhere. God is N-O-W-H-E-R-E. By a slight emphasis, you can change the whole implication. God is *now here*. God is "nowhere" in the sense that God is nowhere to be found, not a person, not a place, not even a being that can be related to in some distinct place in the universe by some special, unique process. God is Presence, all presence, all present, now here. The only way I can know God is to know that expression of God. The only way I can know God is to know myself and to find the depth of myself. I will suddenly find myself at the point when the Allness of God is expressing itself or himself or, if you will, herself at the point of me. The Allness expressing as an eachness.

## THAT WHICH EVOLVES COMES OUT OF THAT WHICH IS INVOLVED

We think of God as the creator. This has been one of the great problems in religious tradition: God who created the heavens and the earth using the first seven days of creation in the first chapter of Genesis. The mind immediately runs to a thought of a superhuman being, a giant Mr. Fix-It. When Genesis says, "In the beginning, God …" we tend to think in terms of time and space. *In the beginning* means where it all started, way back there somewhere, eons ago.

We also get into arguments of whether that was 4,000 years ago or 400 million years ago. In the beginning, way back there, God created the heavens and the earth, so immediately, we tend to think of this giant, Michelangelo-like God sitting on a cloud a lá Marc Connelly's *The Green Pastures*, patting his tummy, feeling very bored with himself and saying, "Well, I guess I'll create me a world," just on a whim, just to have something to do. He reaches out into the void and waves his hands around, and through *presto chango*, out comes the planet Earth. Out comes the sun and the moon and out comes humankind and all the animals to populate the earth and so forth. The whole thing is a rather whimsical, symbolical expression of something that appears to make great sense, if we care to get into it, in a relative sense.

The point is we have the feeling that God created everything out of nothing. Now, I'm sure that this is something that many of us have as a fixation in consciousness, that God created everything out of nothing. A little child in Sunday school can possibly set us all straight by at least asking a deeper question, "Who made God?" If God created everything out of nothing, then where does God come in? But God doesn't come in because God doesn't go out. The universe doesn't come in, although its manifestation may, because the universe, in terms of the whole of things, can never go out.

Again, this may be shattering and shocking and mind-blowing, and I hope it is. As a child, I used to blow my mind sitting down with a young Catholic friend of mine. We'd sit on the curb and we would talk about the creation of the world—fantastic things for kids. I think I was about 9 years old at the time, talking about how the world was created. The thing that would always stick in our mind was this question: What happened before the creation? God created the heavens and the earth, but what about before that, when there was nothing? Can you imagine that? It's beyond imagination, and it just used to have us reeling. We would lie back on the grass and stare at the sky. We would almost knock ourselves out trying to think this through.

See, this has been the problem, creating something out of nothing. Something has come to me, and there's nothing original about it at all, but it's a way of resolving my 9-year-old self's dilemma. What has come to me very strongly is that the creation is not forming things out of nothing. This is why we're saying in the beginning, Allness. Not the beginning void, but in the beginning, Allness. All things have unfolded out of everything's potential. That which *evolves* comes out of that which is *involved*.

This is so fundamental, and again, don't take it too lightly: That which evolves always comes out of that which is involved. The involution (involvement) is infinite, which means the evolution is also infinite and eternal. The universe has no end in terms of time. It has no end because it has no beginning. More correctly, the beginning refers, basically, to a *foundation* and the end refers to an *intention*.

See, we think of the beginning and the end in terms of space-time. Something starts and something stops. *In the beginning* does not refer to year zero. It refers to what the philosopher would call the ground, the basis, the fundamental principle. If you sit in a laboratory and you're going to put together some chemicals and develop some sort of a process that's going to be very helpful to science or medicine or nutrition, the beginning is not when you first put the chemicals together in the test tubes. The beginning is the fundamental laws upon which you build your experiment— its foundation or ground. "In the beginning, God …" means the foundation, the principle, the process, the evolutionary creation, evolving itself into a creative expression. God now stands out or is expressed by this process, but did *not* come out of nothing.

## You Are the Expression of the Creative Process

This is so important because it helps us to understand certain things about ourselves. It's the key to healing. It's the key to overcoming. It's the key to the demonstration of prosperity. No matter what you need or desire, there's a counterpart Allness involved within you and within all things. You can never really be separated from this because you are the expression of the infinite creative process expressing itself as you.

You may not see yourself in relationship to the Allness, the wholeness, yet you are whether you know it or not. You will experience the degree to which you know it, so if you see yourself in part, then you have a partial experience. Even in the midst of that partial experience, which may be in terms of not enough money or not a good job or poor relationships or physical difficulties or deformity, in every case, this is a partial expression or an experience of the expression of the wholeness, of the Allness. Even in the midst of that partial expression, there is a counterpart Allness. That's the key to spiritual healing. This is why I say so often that there's an Allness even within your illness. There is a whole of substance even within a feeling and experience of poverty. There's an Allness because you live in a universe that is whole.

This is one of the great ideas of our time. It's so important that we relate this in our metaphysical system. We're told to be still and know that I am God. Be still and know that I am a fulfilling expression of the Allness of God, that I am whole, that I am complete, that there's a force, a process within me that's everseeking to express itself because that's what life is. It's constant in its expression of possibilities. If I can know this, if I can establish my identity within it, then I'm in the flow of the evolution. In terms of healing and growth and limitless possibilities, they are available to each of us because our wholeness is the fundamental principle that has been demonstrated. That which God has done, God can do.

## WHEREVER SPIRIT IS, THE WHOLE OF SPIRIT MUST BE

You see, this Allness is totally present. I refer often to Judge Thomas Troward's concept, which I refer to as the unity principle. I think it's one of the great metaphysical ideas that have ever been expressed. He says, "Wherever Spirit is at all, the whole of Spirit must be." Now, the word *Spirit* here is used as a synonym for God or, if you will, for the universe, because I see the universe as a synonym for God. "Wherever Spirit is at all, the whole of Spirit must be," because Spirit is wholeness. But he says because Spirit is omnipresent, the whole of Spirit must be present in its entirety at every point in space at the same time.

You see, because we've related to God out of a space-time frame of reference, we've tended to think of God as being present here, as the U.S. government would have an embassy in a foreign country. It has its presence there, you see, so we think that God has presence here, as an emissary of life and substance to help us, to guide us, to direct us. That's limiting because there's a tendency to also think that God has an awful lot of things to do other than take care of us. He's got to take care of what's going on in the Middle East. He's got to take care of the question of crime in the streets. He's got a lot to take care of. How can God take care of me? We tend to think that the Presence is kind of thin. This mindset is very limited.

In the unity principle, Troward outlines that the whole of Spirit must be present in its entirety at every point in space at the same time. The whole ball of wax, everything, totality. The whole of infinite mind is present at the point of my mind. There's no point in asking God to give you an idea because God doesn't have ideas. God is mind, and God doesn't give ideas. God is the Allness of the infinite mind process, which is present in its entirety at every point in space, which means right here *as* your mind.

Your mind is open as an extension of, an expression of, an identity within the all-knowing, infinite Mind of God. It's nowhere else. There's nowhere to go. You can't go to a shrine and get any closer. You can't go to church and get any closer. I'm not against going to church because it will help you get more involved with this process, but only if you understand the process here. You don't go there to get it and leave it behind when you're done. You take it with you because you always have it with you. As I always say, God is in a church simply because people are there. Of course, that's being a little whimsical, but the point is God is here because you're here, as far as you're concerned. That's vitally important. You can't get out of it, but wherever Spirit is at all, the whole must be. The whole spirit, the whole of healing, the whole of substance, the whole of guidance, the whole of creativity is present because you're present.

The Holy Spirit is present and can't be absent because it is all presence, everywhere present, constant. It is present for me because I am present in awareness, because I know it, because I experience it. You don't get it from a group. You don't get it from a shrine. You don't get it from a person. It comes from the awareness of your own experience, which can never be separated from you.

## GOD AS PRINCIPLE, PRESSING ITSELF OUT INTO LIFE

H. Emilie Cady, in her book *Lessons in Truth*, makes a statement I think we need to discuss. She says, "God is not a being with qualities or attributes, but He is the good itself coming into expression as life, love, power, wisdom, etc." *He is the good itself coming into expression as life, love, power, and wisdom.* In other words, and this again is shattering to some of us: God is not loving. God is a loving God. God is not loving because the moment we talk about God as loving, we tend to [see] the anthropomorphic Michelangelo-like God sitting up on a cloud somewhere with His heart beaming out, saying, "Oh, I love you all down there so dearly, as long as you're good, but I'm not going to love you very much if you don't go to church." I say, God is not loving. God *is* love. See the difference?

This is why German theologian Meister Eckhart said, "I don't thank God for loving me, because He can't help Himself." What does that mean? The Bible says it first: "Behold, I have loved you with an everlasting love" (Jeremiah 31:3). There's no way God can express anything other than love for you. After all, you are the expression of the Infinite pressing itself out as you. If God is love, then you are love in potential. God is not loving. God is love. This is so important. We're now thinking in terms of principle.

Similarly, God is not wise. When we see God as wise and wonderful and just God, we tend to see him with all the ideas, who will help me if I just approach him in the right way. Yet God is *not* wise. God is the Allness of wisdom, Allness that is present in its entirety at every point in space at the same time, so God is present where I am, right here, right now.

God is not a healer. Again, we tend to think God will heal us if we pray to him. Again, let me free you of that, or at least shock you a little bit. God isn't going to heal you of anything. God doesn't heal because God is the Allness of life. Healing is the experience of leaving the darkness and coming into the light, leaving the confusion of human consciousness and coming into the Allness, which is always present. The Allness of infinite life is present even within the illness. So God is not a healer. He doesn't look down upon you and say, "Well, you're sick, but you're a good person and I like you very much, so I'm going to take this illness away from you." God doesn't take illness away from anybody, nor does God put illness into anyone, which belies a lot of traditional religious thought. We talk about suffering as if it's God's will and then it's my place to accept it. No, not at all.

The will of God must always be the ceaseless longing of the Creator to express itself in that which it has created. It's a constancy. It's a force that is always seeking to press itself out into visibility as life, as wholeness, as success. Our need is not to get God to do the job. That's like saying, "Let's get gravity on the job. I'm going to step off a curb. Let's be sure that gravity knows about it." Gravity doesn't know about it. Gravity is. Gravity is a force that dominates all aspects of this universe. There's no way to get out of it. Gravity doesn't have knowledge of people stepping up on high places and going down, or airplanes going up and then down, and so forth. Gravity knows nothing about this.

This is why the Bible says the eyes of God are too pure to behold iniquity (Habakkuk 1:13). The purity is Allness, totality, completion, the Infinite Mind. We're dealing with principle. If God were a healer, you'd have to call ahead for office hours. You'd get a notice to come back in two weeks when they could fit you in or when it's his whim or his desire or maybe he wills it, or maybe he loves you a little more that time than he does this time. Forgive my whimsy!

God is not a healer. God is life, and the whole of life is present in its entirety at every point in space at the same time. Now, doesn't that make a difference? Get that into your consciousness. There's nowhere to go for healing. Wherever you are, the Allness of healing life is present. It is not to get God to do something for you, but to be still and know that I am God, to get back to the beginning, to the roots, the foundation. In the beginning, Allness, totality. If we could just realize this and work with this understanding, it would make such a difference in our lives.

## You Are a Whole Eachness of That Principle

The mystical Truth, again, is that I am an eachness. Maybe that point is oversimplified. I am an eachness within the Allness of God and the full power of the whole, or the Allness, is present within every cell of the eachness. The totality of the infinite healing process is present in the tiniest cell of my body. Isn't that a wonderful thing to know? In biologist Edmund Sinnott's book, *The Biology of the Spirit*, he senses this process in nature, and he describes it as a total, all-inclusive process. He says, "Somehow, there must be present in the plant's living stuff, immanent in all its parts, something that represents the natural configuration of the whole as a norm to which its growth conforms, a goal toward which development is invariably directed. This insistent fact confronts us everywhere in biology."

I might add this insistent fact confronts everywhere in human life, too, because that's the thing that helps us to understand what God is. Not G-O-D, not the floating literary symbol, not something or someone that sits off there somewhere in the universe, but God Presence. God is totality. God is that which expresses in me as what Sinnott calls the natural configuration of the whole, the whole in the part, the whole pattern. To put it another way, one of the medieval mystics, St. Augustine, is attributed to saying, "God is a circle whose center is everywhere and whose circumference is nowhere."

One of my students once corrected this, saying that God is not a circle, but God is a sphere, which is three-dimensional. The circle is two-dimensional. Let's say then that God is a sphere whose center is everywhere and whose circumference is nowhere. When you first read this or hear this, it sounds so logical. You could almost draw a picture of it. God is a sphere whose center is everywhere and whose circumference is nowhere. The center is here, but there's no circumference.

What this means is that any point in the universe is the heart of the universe. The universe is not to be understood as a geographical expanse but as a cosmic consciousness, which means the Infinite is present at any point and there is a whole in every part. The whole universe is present at the point where you are. Where you are is the very heart of it, the center of it, not somewhere in the outer reaches. The whole universe is present as you, and you are the very center of it because it is centered at the point where you are.

The seed can become a tree because the tree is in the seed. That makes sense, doesn't it? The egg can become a bird because the bird is in the egg, but look at it in terms of yourself. You can become what you really desire because your divine potential or, as Paul would call it, the Christ, is within you always. Not some of the time, not if you take a class and acquire more knowledge. Human potential studies don't put potentiality in anyone, but they help you to understand the potential that is always present.

You can become what you really desire to be, not because of some divine intervention, not because of some newfangled metaphysical system you're going to learn, not because someone puts his hands upon you and works some spiritual magic. You can do this because your divine potential, the Christ of you, is always present within you as the Allness of the infinite process expressing as you. This is an important principle by which you can deal with life.

To put it this way, whatever is, is whole, whether you can see that wholeness or experience it or not. English poet Robert Browning puts it this way. He says, "On the earth, the broken arc. In the heavens, the perfect round." You may see a lot of broken arcs around. You may see a lot of deprived and depraved lives. You may see a lot of frustrated people. You may see a lot of perverse, even criminally insane, people. In every case, you are seeing but a broken arc of a perfect whole. You cannot get a sense of God's universal system as long as you're thinking of a broken arc. The broken arc is but a dim perception of wholeness. This is why we say there's no such thing as totally bad people. There's no such thing as incurable illness. There's no such thing as impossibility in any realm of life because whatever is, is whole.

That doesn't mean we just immediately step from the partial to the whole. Most of us know there's a great deal of spiritual growth involved, one step at a time. The principle is the thing we're concerned about.

## THE EFFECT OF YOUR CONSCIOUSNESS

If you begin with the principle that you might as well face it, then you're done before you begin. If you think of yourself as only human, then you've totally ruled out the idea of the divine process of you, which is the reality of you.

I think a lot of folks have settled for less than their better selves, usually out of conformity, usually out of rationalization, usually out of an attitude of self-limitation. "This is just the way I am." It's not the way you are, but if you think it's the way you are, then it's the way you will be as far as you're concerned. That's what consciousness is. You can expand your awareness and see yourself in a larger context. Suddenly, you open up to a whole new universe for yourself, and so Jesus then says, "All things are possible to them that believe" (Mark 9:23). All things, can you believe that? *All things.*

You start where you are and say, "Well, that means I can get a better job." Of course, but it also means we can have peace in the world. It means we can have an interrelationship of people in harmony and order and love. All things are possible. Perhaps not today, perhaps not tomorrow because it takes us a while to wake up, but all things are possible. Whatever is, is whole, whether you see that wholeness or whether you experience that wholeness or not. That's a marvelous principle to relate to in terms of yourself.

Now it's so important to get to the realization of God as principle. Not as a person, not as present somewhere, but God as a principle. People say, "Well, that's too cold and impersonal for me." As some have said, "They've taken my Lord away." The fact is, they may take your Lord away if your Lord has been someone who sits off there somewhere in the universe. They may have taken away your anthropomorphic God but then given you Presence. Remember, Ralph Waldo Emerson says a beautiful thought that's always been inspiring to me: "When you've broken with the God of tradition and ceased from the God of the intellect, then God fires you with His presence."

When you stop dealing with, relating to, pleading and supplicating from something/someone out there, and get involved in the realization of the wholeness of life, then suddenly you become immersed in the presence of God. No longer do you believe *in* God. Instead, you have a believing attitude that is based on the presence of God. You're not believing in the floating literary symbol. You don't believe *in* it—something that's this symbolic gesture of the whole—but you believe, and your believing attitude is based upon the realization of the activity of God, which is present.

It's like saying, "I believe in gravity." Someone once came to Emerson and said, "Mr. Emerson, I believe in the universe." He said, "By God, you'd better." You could go out on the street and say, "I believe in gravity. I believe in gravity." Okay, if you do, then look where you're going because gravity is functioning. Better to believe not *in* God but believe *from* a consciousness of

God. That's the important thing that counts, you see. It's not a matter of just saying, "I believe. I believe. I believe." Some people say, "Oh, I love God. I love God so much. Oh, I just love God." I'm always a little bit suspicious of a person who says this, because as the Bible said, "If you say you love God and hate your brother, you're a liar" (1 John 4:20). When someone says, "I love God. I love God. I love God," you may want to look and see if they love everybody. Obviously, you'll find some deficiencies. Don't talk about it, do it. Love, but don't love God—love from the consciousness of the Allness of love. You have the infinite potential of love ever with you, and you can love out of that consciousness.

I believe. I have a believing attitude. I believe in the possibilities of people. I believe in my potential in my work. I have a believing attitude that relates me with all things in a positive way because I know, in the beginning, Allness. Not the beginning way back there, but the foundation. I am an expression of the Allness of God, which is ever-present.

## THE PRACTICE OF THE PRESENCE OF GOD

Brother Lawrence, a 17th-century Carmelite monk, coined the phrase "the practice of the presence of God" many hundreds of years ago. It's a term that has been very interesting and very helpful to a lot of people. I love it myself, but you see, to practice the presence does not necessarily mean feeling something special or receiving flashes of sight or sound or having these intuitive senses of the infinite process or cosmic awareness. It doesn't necessarily imply meditating throughout a long period of time. This is not essentially what is implied by the practice of the presence. We can make it seem too complicated and thus totally eliminate the possibility of practice.

A doctor practices medicine. Does that mean he sits lotus-like on a pillow and gets these cosmic revelations before he dispenses his pills to people? It doesn't mean that at all. When it says he "practices medicine," this is not an emotional experience, it's simply telling you how he makes his living. He practices medicine. Practical metaphysics, or the practice of the presence of God, is relating all things to the God process and identifying a channel for the Allness. It's getting ourselves in tune and working out of that consciousness.

To practice the presence is to live constantly as if you believe that the Allness of God were present in all its totality, at every point in space. This means it's present in you, in every experience of your life and every function of your body. That's the practice of the presence.

Even the piano enthusiast goes to the piano every once in a while and practices her scales and deludes herself into believing she's learning to be a piano player. She may become one, but basically, she never really becomes an artist at the piano. To be that artist requires playing the piano until she gets interrelated with the rhythmic laws of music and relates them with her physical skills to the keyboard or the piano. Then something happens, something beautiful, a transcendent awareness.

The practice of the presence of God has very little to do with those few moments when you study or you have your meditation. Obviously, that's a part of it, but it's so much more than that. The practice of the presence means what you do with your life, like the practice of medicine is what the doctor does for a living. "What do you do?" "Oh, I practice the presence." Do you? Are you practicing it when you worry? Are you practicing when you're fuming and fretting because you missed a subway? Are you practicing the presence when you go off to work and you just feel terribly anxious because the boss has asked you to come in and have a talk with him'? Are you *really* practicing the presence?

To practice the presence is to live constantly as if you really believed that the Allness of God, the divine potential for wholeness, were present within you. You believe this with every part and parcel of your life, every concern of you, every experience of your involvement with people, in every function of your body—to believe it and act as if you believe it. That takes some time, so when we talk about practical metaphysics, we imply very seriously that there's a lot of practice to be done.

## HOW TO PRACTICE THE PRESENCE

Let me give you a little homework assignment. This is not something to write down, not a lot of words to memorize, but it's a project of involvement and thinking, meditating, and relating. Remember, the Allness refers to totality, and the beginning doesn't mean time, it means foundation. In the beginning, Allness, means right where you are right now, the most important thing to you, the most important thing about your life and your involvement is that you are living in an expression of the Allness of the divine potential, and it's constant. The totality of the universe is present where you are. This is the big starting point. The Allness of mind, the Allness of substance. You may have a desire to make more money, but right now, you rest upon the principle of all-sufficient substance.

It's like a person talking out a problem: two plus two. He's going to try and make the two plus two come out as four, but the beginning is the principle in which the four is immanent even in the two plus two. When would you put two plus two on the paper? Before you draw a line, put a plus sign. It already implies four, you see. This is in the beginning, Allness. In the beginning, at the heart and root of your life, the whole process of the infinite activity is present as you. The important thing is to take some time, especially at the beginning of the day, and as many times during the day as you want, to come back to it and remember to make a practice of starting all things at the beginning. Not in the point of time, but at the foundation, the realization.

The whole of mind, the whole of infinite creativity, is in you and expressing as you in all your plans, all your projects, all your relationships. Before you go into a relationship, before you go into the office, before you start off in the morning walking down the street, before you do anything, quietly, quickly turn to yourself within and identify as an expression, an eachness, within the Allness that is God. You are the expression of this divine life process. This is to get the most out of your experience.

The whole of life is present in every part of your body as a healing process, sustaining you, blessing you, changing, healing, renewing. If you're having any kind of a physical problem, take a moment to close your eyes and just get very still. Certain phrases and metaphysical treatments may be helpful, but basically, in the beginning, just be still and know Allness. Forget about the limitation of the eachness. Forget about the thought of the physical difficulty, of the pain, the confusion. Just let yourself quietly realize Allness, wholeness, totality, completely. The Allness of the universe pressing itself out into visibility almost as if it's a light of focus that is centered right at the point where you are. Just get that vision and consciousness.

If you are struggling personally or professionally, get the sense that the whole of substance is present in your affairs as prosperity and success. The whole of it, not some of it. Not a little bit more in the paycheck, but the whole of substance, the whole of substance of all the universe is present in its entirety at the point where you are. The need is to let go of the limitation, let go of "I only have so much." Let go of the feeling and fear of limitation.

So it is in your relationships with people. Instead of wishing you had more love in your life or more harmonious relationships, let it go and take a moment to be still and get the feeling of being centered totally and completely in the Allness of infinite love. Feel the love that is constantly loving you because it can't do anything else but love you. As you allow this love to recharge and regenerate you from within, you become more loving and a radiant, attractive force for love to draw forth that kind of a relationship with other people. Take time to know Allness. Take time to know the beginning and for realizing not a point in time, but a principle, a foundation, a presence, an activity, Allness, wholeness, completeness, totality, transcendence. In the beginning, Allness.

## MEDITATION

*Let's just be still for a moment. Let's just get the feeling that what we've talked about so far is totally preparatory. We've empowered* words, words, words, words. Words really are meaningless except that they direct us to consciousness, feeling, awareness. Let it all go now. Let the creative process come into a living experience right here where you are. Think about the first words of the Bible, "In the beginning, God ..." We're simply saying, in the beginning, Allness.

At the foundation of you, your life, and your experience, is the wholeness of the universal process expressing itself as you. Just think of yourself for a moment as being the central point of focus of light. Light is in sharp focus, and you never lose it. You are a point of light in the infinite light of God. You are an expression of love in the limitless love of the Infinite. You're an experience of wholeness and health and the activity of the Allness of healing life. You are a flow of substance within the all sufficiency of infinite supply, and this flowing pours through you, as you, and it feels good. Don't let yourself wonder how. Don't question who made God. Don't think in terms of what was there before. There was nothing. Let all of these human thoughts go. Just feel your oneness with the Allness of the Infinite. In the beginning, Allness.

So we begin. Not so much a beginning in time, although it can be that, too, but that it begins here in terms of a principle that is realized here. In the beginning, Allness. Thinking in terms of what lies before you, the work you'll be involved in tomorrow, the physical experience, even the diagnosis and the prognosis of doctors who have judged your physical form. In every case, in the beginning, Allness, Allness, Allness, Allness. Remember, wherever you are, the Allness of God is present, and the Allness of God is present because you're present. You are always and in all ways an eachness within the Allness that is God.

# 2

## DIVINITY OF MAN

### WE MUST BEGIN WITH OURSELVES AND OUR SENSES

IN THE FIRST lesson, we dealt with what we called *in the beginning*, the onus, trying to build a foundation of reality. Hopefully, as we create the foundation for a practical metaphysician, we are trying to avoid the intellectualizations that we normally attach to it. It's easy to build a cosmology or metaphysical awareness of the universe, and have reams of definitions, intellectual propositions, treatments, affirmations, and yet have ourselves totally on the outside looking in. Quite often we read about the very complicated cosmological studies of humans, life, and the universe—some of the esoteric treatises and libraries abound with them. We see pictures of the cosmology of the universe. We see pictures of the various levels of consciousness and the seven steps to eternity, and so forth.

These are very interesting and very reasonable. Obviously, some of them can be helpful to certain people and certain levels of consciousness. However, at some point, this is not what we learn, or this is not what is left over because if this is all that remains and we're still on the outside, we're still looking at a picture in a book. We're still trying to define or relate to something that is beautiful and wonderful and infinite, and yet it's still out there somewhere.

To put it simply, I say we must put ourselves in the picture and build ourselves into the structure. The Greeks had a phrase for it, as they so often did. Inscribed over the entrance to the Temple of the Delphi are the words, "Know thyself." It's important, somewhere along the early stages in our quest to understand life and the universe, that we begin with ourselves, that we affirm, very simply, very easily: *I exist. I'm here. I think, I feel, I cease, I perceive, I am.* That's a starting point.

Just think about the physical body, for instance. As we say often, "You do not live as a body. Your body is not you. You have a body." The "you" that has the body is far transcendent to the body, but the body is a very important part of self-expression. At a certain level of consciousness, you express in and as this body, and this is where you are right now. Whatever else this body is, it is. You can define it, you can describe it, you can give a definition of the anatomical structures, you can have a biological insight into what is going on within it, but the most important thing is that it is.

It is flesh. It is sensual. It is beautiful. It is. The senses play a great role. We say again that man is not a sensual creature. You are not senses. You are not sensual. You are not sex, but you have these areas of expression through which the life process flows as a conduit. The senses are very important to you. They help you to provide a link with your environment—and it's yours—but you understand the senses before we try to deny them or to say, "There are no such things as physical experiences. I am a spiritual creature."

Before we try to discipline them, we need to know how they function, and to know ourselves in relationship to them. Through our senses we become aware of things around us. We become aware of people. We become aware of our environment. We become aware of the world in which we live. We see colors. We hear sounds. We smell fragrances. We taste delicacies. We touch warm and cool things, and all of these have life and vitality because we sense them.

## WE ARE ENVIRONED BY THE SENSES

Unless we begin with the realization that I exist, that I'm here, that I sense, that I feel, then we tend only to look out into our environment from the outside. The environment becomes something totally separate from us, something that is either hostile, or something that is not friendly, but there's nothing that you can do about it.

The fact is, you can change your environment because your environment is your sensual awareness of that which environs you. You are environed by your own feelings, by your own thought. Everything that happens out here happens in you, and you can change what happens in you. Thus you can change what happens out here.

It's a simple thing but such a helpful one. Otherwise, we tend to say: "Well, what are we going to do about it?" "That's the way things are." "You can't change anything." Your environment and experience through the senses, then, is a part of you. It's a part of your life.

The colors of the rainbow are gathered from colorless light, so you see beautiful auras of color because you see them. They exist in your mind. There's no world of color and sound without the interpreting mind. For instance, a dog may hear all the notes of the symphony, but it doesn't hear a symphony. That's why it howls. It's painful. It just hears all sorts of sounds, but it doesn't hear music because music is in the mind. It's in the listener.

A symphonic orchestra would be creating dissonances and a cacophony that we wouldn't be able to listen to unless we had a musical mind, unless we could understand. Hence, the audience becomes a very important part of the experience. Without us, there's no music.

Philosopher Alfred North Whitehead comments on this. He says, "Nature gets credit which in truth should be reserved for ourselves—the rose for its scent, the nightingale for its song, the sun for its radiance." He also says, "The poets are mistaken. They should address their lyrics to themselves and turn them into odes of self-congratulation on the excellence of the human mind. Nature is a dull affair, soundless, senseless, colorless, merely the hurrying of material, endlessly, meaningless." It has meaning because you have meaning, and because you read meaning into it, you exist, and you're there.

This gives a new insight into ourselves. We need occasionally, not egotistically but in a great sense of appreciation, to reach behind our back and give ourselves a nice little pat. You're all right. You're all right because you exist, because you see things, and because you have the ability to see them in all sorts of diverse ways.

Shakespeare had this tremendous appreciation of man, as in his *Hamlet*, he says, "What a piece of work is man. How noble in reason, how infinite in faculty. In form and moving, how express and admirable. In action how like an angel. In apprehension, how like a god." Of course, this talks about the height of man's consciousness, the great spiritual potential that is within man. It senses something about the hidden mystery of God and man that Paul calls, "Christ in you, your hope of glory."

## Man as I AM-age and Likeness of God

It's a beautiful realization, but unfortunately the full sense of these words has been predominantly lost throughout Christian tradition because we have been led to believe that Paul refers here to Jesus, when he says, "Christ in you, your hope of glory" (Colossians 1:27). We assume that means, "Jesus in you is the hope of your life." That isn't what Paul had in mind at all and misunderstands the divine possibility that he's suggesting.

Christ, you see, which he refers to, is not Jesus at all. Jesus discovered this dimension of the Christ, and therefore he was called, figuratively, "Jesus Christ," but Christ is the God possibility within every person. It's your hope of overcoming, it's your hope of healing, your hope of growing and doing the greater things that Jesus promised you can do. It's a depth of you, not something that can be added on, or put into, or something that you get just by believing in somebody else, even in Jesus. It's that which is the reality of you from the very beginning, the very foundation of your life.

The Book of Genesis says, "God created man in his own image, and after his likeness" (Genesis 1:26, 27). This may be the most majestic statement in the Bible. The image is you and as God sees you, and the likeness is that which you must work out in your consciousness and outform in your body and affairs. In other words, as we say so often, within you is the unborn possibility of limitless life. This is the image, and yours is the privilege of giving birth to it. This is the likeness. This is something that is your responsibility.

It is your destiny to outform or produce a likeness in the divine image within. The divine image has new meaning if you think of it in a loose interpretation, "I AM-age." The I AM-age. Remember when Moses asked the voice within, "Who should I say sent me?" The voice came back and said, "I AM that I AM." The I AM is God, but it is the I AM God experienced within us. It is what we referred to in Chapter 1 as, "Your eachness within the Allness." The I AM-age is the divine possibility, the divine potential, the divine depth within you that is always present no matter where you are in consciousness, no matter where you are in experience. It's your destiny to produce the likeness, the manifestation of this I AM-age, so that you can come to experience an I AM-ness in your relationships and your life. This is exactly what Jesus did. This gives us a new insight into what is going on in the New Testament studies. Theologians have said that Jesus was God become man, but Jesus knew that God already had become man when God first breathed the breath of life into his own image, and it became a living soul.

The difference between Jesus and you and I was not one of the mere manner of his birth, it was not because of some special dispensation, it was not just because of some mere potentiality that was in him but not in others—the difference was in the awareness of that potential. The difference was in the consciousness of that I AM-age.

## ORTHODOXY RESPONDS TO GNOSTICISM

Orthodoxy has preached that man is a poor, miserable sinner. This is something that needs to be carefully considered. This idea of man as a poor, miserable sinner is a deviously—I emphasize *deviously*—developed dogma that was created by early Christian teachers to offset the heresy of monasticism.

It was a political ploy, if you want to put it in that basis because there were those who were seeing Jesus and his teaching in an entirely different way. The gnostics, who were mainly centered around Egypt, were students of what they considered themselves in those days to be the new insight in. They were seeing the Christian teaching in an esoteric sense, not through the personality of Jesus, and of course they were a great threat to the personality cult of Jesus that was being developed.

The Christian traditionalists developed this dogma that Jesus was God and that man was a miserable sinner. This was to make the total separation between Jesus and man. He was not human. He was God. Totally God. Very God.

## Orthodoxy Misuses Psalm 51

In support of this concept of man as a miserable sinner, they took one of the psalms of David, Psalm 51: "I was shaped in iniquity, and in sin did my mother conceive me."

Yet these words are totally out of context. You have to read them in the full context of how the psalm is expressed.

The fact is that there's much in the Bible that was never intended to be a pattern for observation or something to emulate. David, when he wrote the psalms, wrote in many different levels of consciousness. You can't just read all of Psalms and say, "This is the voice of God speaking," because David wrote, as all poets do and all songwriters do, out of the expression of their emotions, and one's emotions are not always on the high place. David may have sung, "The Lord is my shepherd, I shall not want" (Psalm 23:1), but he also sang, in Psalm 22 right before it, "Oh Lord, oh Lord, why art thou so far from the voice of my groaning?"

This was a downbeat consciousness. He was expressing his feelings, and that day he wasn't feeling very well. Psalm 51, we know today, was written when David was experiencing a soliloquy over the great confusion and the remorse and the regret of his affair with Bathsheba.

David was a highly evolved person, but he was still human; he had aspirations, but he wasn't always able to live up to them. One day he was sitting in his palace, looking out across the wall to a neighboring area where he saw Bathsheba taking a bath. Immediately he fell in love with her as the human sense often does. Then he arranged to have the husband of Bathsheba sent off into the battle lands to be destroyed so that he could have Bathsheba for his wife, and so she became the wife of David.

This is not exactly the kind of thing worthy of emulation, but we're not making judgments on David. We are saying that when David wrote Psalm 51 he was singing out of remorse, "Oh God, I wish I had never been born." Again, this is what is in the back of the words, "I was shaped in iniquity, and in sin did my mother conceive me." It was a psalm of despair in which David was commiserating.

## THE TRUE TEACHING OF JESUS

The point is, unfortunately, Christian tradition has supported this concept of the miserable sinner nature of man and the divinity of Jesus, which totally loses the full thrust of that which Jesus had to give to every one of us as a teaching.

The heart of Jesus' teachings was not the depravity of man but the divinity of man. The heart of Jesus' teachings was the I AM-ness of every individual. Jesus discovered this principle of divine sense. He discovered his own divine image, and he fulfilled the personal requirement of living it out into expression fully and completely, demonstrated in his own experience. His ministry was devoted to the "repeatability of the Christ." That's a phrase that some don't like because of their traditional backgrounds, but it's a very important one. "Nothing shall be impossible unto you," he said. *Nothing!*

He went on to say, "There are the things that I do, you can do, too, and greater things shall you do if you have faith" (John 14:12). This certainly doesn't set him apart, you see, but it says that there's a divine possibility within every person. Jesus discovered it. This was his main role. He demonstrated it. He spent his life teaching other people how to experience it and showing the greater things that could happen if you do fulfill it and give it expression.

Jesus said, "Be ye perfect as your father in heaven is perfect" (Matthew 5:48). Why would he say this if he did not believe that every person contained within them the same unborn possibility of perfection as he did, and that as Jesus himself had given birth to it, so could anyone give birth to it by commitment, by growth, by dedication, by work, and by practice?

## WE MUST BEGIN BY KNOWING OUR CHRIST POTENTIAL

Truth study, for many people, is motivated by a deep feeling of spiritual inferiority. Let's face it, this is quite often the thing that motivates us when we begin to study Truth. We want to be more. We want to be better. We want to overcome the stigma of the presumed sinfulness of man. This is a motivation that is felt within all persons, so quite often, the quest for Truth becomes a program of seeking, reaching, and straining to get and become. "I want to become spiritual."

Let me disillusion you. There's no way that you can ever become "spiritual." There's no way that you can ever be more spiritual than you already are because being spiritual is your nature. It's not something that you can study and acquire as a result of techniques, or as a result of classroom experiences. There's no way that through reading this or any other book you can become spiritual. You *are* spiritual. That's the fundamental Truth. This is your nature. This is the I AM. You are created in God's image and likeness. Deep at the heart of you there is a spiritual tone that is absolutely, unequivocally the reality of you. You can never be anything less.

Without the knowledge and experience of the Christ Potential within, we're lost. We tend, as modern psychology used to, to think of the brain as a sealed compartment. We need to know that becoming spiritual is a matter of waking up, becoming aware of I AM. Without this, we begin to wonder about certain evidences of great possibilities that we see around us in life, and we think, "Well, it's because of ESP," or "It's because she's a child prodigy," or "It's because he's a genius," but we certainly have great evidence that the normal human limit is often exceeded to a great extent.

Again, we're conditioned through our educational background to believe that this is simply an evidence of the bewildering complexity of the brain and the enormous number of brain cells that are almost sufficient to explain things, even to cover an explanation for paranormal phenomena. But I find that insufficient. Something more is needed to understand life and to understand ourselves.

I love the explanation given by Professor William Bateson in the British Society for Scientific Research. He says, "We are finding now, beyond doubt, that the gifted and the geniuses of [humankind] are due not so much to something added to the ordinary person, but instead are due to factors which in the normal person inhibit the development of these gifts. They are now without doubt to be looked upon as releases of powers normally suppressed."

This is a very important insight because there is a particular genius within you. It doesn't mean that every person can do what other people do or become what other people become, because we're not in a popularity contest. We're not trying to be better than other people, but we're trying, as the ancient mystics said, to be better than our former self. The great competition is like a golfer on the golf course. He's not really competing with other people. He's competing with himself. He's trying to better himself, to improve his skills.

So it is with all of our relationships in life, so important that the great key is to know that each of us has more within us, and growth is experiencing more of it, releasing the powers that are normally suppressed.

There is within every person the potential for what American philosopher Henry David Thoreau calls, "The license of a higher order of being." That potential is within you. The license was always there. You don't have to somehow get God in the right mood so that he will say, "Well, it's my will and you can now do it," because God has already done for all of us what God can do when he included us in his image-likeness. The potential is there, all built in, according to our uniqueness. Ours is the privilege of understanding it and releasing it and giving birth to it.

You have the capacity to be more, to reach higher, to achieve the very depths and heights of your potential and God Self. It's always present, and ours is the privilege to work at it today.

This takes away many of our excuses. We're just full of excuses. We say, "I would like to do this, but I don't have the time. I haven't had the right background, and I wish that I could understand some of these great things of Truth. It would have been nice if I could have been exposed to Truth when I was a child, but at my age, you know, it's kind of difficult."

The thing is, the license is already issued. You have it in you to do and become all that you have the will to achieve and the vision to perceive. You have the capacity within you right now. The goal is to begin to take steps, to start today, here a little, there a little, to progress. It all begins with how you see yourself and what you think about yourself.

## JESUS DEMONSTRATING THE DESTINY OF MAN

A person like Jesus was endowed with a highly evolved consciousness, but he was still a person.

He was a person demonstrating that we can achieve high evolution if we work at it, if we practice it.

Since he had a highly evolved consciousness, he did things that were amazing to his contemporaries. They couldn't understand him. They could only talk of miracles. They could only talk of divine dispensation. They could only talk of "very God," God doing his great works for us, but they couldn't seem to relate to the fact that this was a highly evolved person doing the kinds of things that represented the license of a higher order of beings. The kind of license that is always a part of the superconscious nature of every person, and of you and me.

What is forgotten so often, and is totally missing in the whole orthodox Christian teaching, is that Jesus was demonstrating, revealing, manifesting, and making real that which ultimately must become normal behavior of a highly evolved human race.

I believe this is where we're going. It's so true that the pessimist is always saying, "Well, I'll tell you where we're going. We're all going to hell in a handbasket." He says, "Look what's going on in the world out here." The fact is, man is an innately divine creature and there's no way that he can escape it. He may postpone it, and we do a very good job of postponing it. We can deviate from it. We can pervert it. We can frustrate it. We can suppress it. But there's no way that we can put it off forever because this is where the human race is going.

You go back through the Bible—the Old Testament and the New Testament—there are those who like to talk about the days when God walked the earth. I say poppycock to that. God walks the earth constantly because God is the Allness that is being expressed as an eachness. Don't let yourself accept the glamorous account of the Old Testament and New Testament times. I've pointed out the experience of David. This is mild compared to what was going on in those days.

The heroes of the Old Testament were merely beginning to experience something of this Allness, and the prophets were those who were far ahead of the people themselves. They were trying to help them understand, but basically we see an evolution of the God process constantly moving through the Bible.

I've told the story of the little boy in Sunday school who had been studying the Old Testament for a year. He learned about this vicious, very vengeful God who wiped out whole cities, and destroyed people, and came down as a bolt of lightning and so forth. Finally, the next course went into a study of the New Testament, about Jesus and a very loving God, the Father presence within, and the little boy remarked, "Boy, God sure got better as he got older, didn't he?"

The fact is God did get better, because God is an extension of our awareness of ourselves. As we come to understand that, we come to understand a larger, deeper, more expanded awareness of the Allness of things. Obviously, we are getting better! It's hard for us to understand this because we are too close to it, but the fact is, the only way you can really understand the nature of humans is to see humans at their highest moments. If you want to see the potential of someone, instead of looking at the criminals in the penitentiary, or the gory news in the newspapers, go to an art gallery or see the human potential in the flowering excellence of the few people who are achieving some greatness. These are the ones who are demonstrating the divine potential in our unfolding.

This is what humanity is all about. We always want to keep ourselves constantly aware of it because this means that Jesus was simply far ahead of his time, demonstrating the tremendous God possibility within us. It implies that the difference between Jesus and each of us is one of inherent spiritual capacity, a difference in the demonstration of potential. Pilate and Jesus were one, in regard to being, but miles apart in regard to the manifestation of that I AM-age. In other words, every person is a potential Christ.

## You Are a Potential Christ

You are a potential Christ. You can only understand yourself or fulfill this thought of humankind, "know thyself," when you come to see that the divine reality of you is the Christ of you. It's the I AM of you, it's the God possibility of you.

Some people won't understand that because they'll think that whenever you use the word *Christ*, you're talking about Jesus, and therefore they'll say that's sacrilegious. As a matter of fact, the word itself is not important. We're not concerned that you say, "Christ in me is my hope of glory," as Paul said, but there's a God potential within me, there's a God Self, there's a reality of me, there's an I AM of me, there's a wholeness of me, even though I may be only expressing part of it.

It may be that "of me" that is usually suppressed, but I can begin to release to it. Wherever you are along the way of your unfoldment, no matter what problems or challenges you face, there is always more in you. The Christ of you, the I AM of you, is your potential for healing, the potential for overcoming, your potential for demonstrating prosperity and success. In Truth, "There is no limit," and as Jesus said, "and greater things than these shall you do."

A lot of metaphysics puts emphasis on the laws of demonstration. Obviously, this is dealing with certain fundamentals of Truth, which is helpful to understand, but quite often this is oversimplified, and as a result we fail to really acknowledge what is being stressed. In other words, the implication is often subtly given that this live demonstration is something you feed into your subconscious mind and then paste over the façade of your human experience to give you a new self-image, a new feeling of joy, new health, new positive power, and so forth. Now you have a new front, behind which quite often is the same scared little person that you always were.

There's a great bit of interest today in human potential, both within metaphysical movements and in the movements of psychology.

Obviously, it's important to understand human potential, but it's important to know that the human potential in you is divine potential. It is the God Self of you, and it's not something you're going to put into you by speaking a lot of affirmations, by invoking some magic law of demonstration. It's not something that you're going to make yourself do, or something that you have not been able to do. All you can do is, as Robert Browning says, "Release your imprisoned splendor," or release the potential Professor Bateson says has normally been suppressed.

## WE CAN ONLY LEARN WHAT WE ALREADY KNOW

The startling truth is you can only become what you already are. That doesn't seem to make sense at first, but when you understand that you're created in God's image and likeness, and that image is the divine potential of you wrapped within your being, then that can never be separated in any way. You can only become what you already are. You can't get a fig out of a maple tree. You can't become something that you do not already have the potential to become. You can only become what you already are. You can only learn what you already know.

You can only learn what you already know. The ancient Greeks had the idea of learning through the word *education*, to draw forth from within. Learning is a drawing forth; learning is recognizing. Learning is what's left when you've forgotten all that you've heard. You may hear a lot of things. As Job says, "I had heard of thee by the hearing of the ear, but now mine eyes see-eth thee" (Job 42:5). I knew about all sorts of things, about this and about that, but I didn't really know.

When you know, you acknowledge, you awaken, you recognize that which you've always known because each of us is an individualized expression of Infinite Mind. We live in a milieu of Mind. We'll be dealing more with that in our next chapter.

In any study, we've had the experience of the light going on over our head, *Ah, I see, yes! I see.* What do you see? Not that you see this, but you see from that which you've always known, and you know this. You've seen this happen often. You're reading in a book, and you think, *It seems as if I've always known that.* The learning process is a recognition of your own identity in the Allness of Infinite Mind, where all things are present.

When you understand this, you come to understand why it is so often that the student exceeds the capacity of the teacher. If this were not so, then for example, a music teacher would be a great composer, but how rarely is a music teacher a great composer? She teaches composing. She teaches the skills. She teaches the techniques, the laws of harmony, counterpoint, orchestration, and all this, but then the student thinks, *Ah, I see.* The student identifies that Allness process and goes beyond the teacher by waking up to that divine process within. It was always there.

If we understand this, then the learning process becomes simplified, and the growing process in our experiences, in our work, in our relationships, is facilitated in a far more remarkable way. We have nothing really to do except to awaken. Remember, Paul says, "Awake now, that sleeper, that Christ may shine upon you" (Ephesians 5:14). In other words, learning is a matter of realizing potentialities, realizing that which has been ourselves from the very beginning of time.

It's not adding to, but it's drawing forth. It's evolving that which has been involved, or as the poet Browning says, "Open out a way whence the imprisoned splendor may escape."

## Our Potential Is Within Us

Your potential, you see, is not something that you can possibly achieve. Your potential is a reality even before you begin to work for it. Your very desire to work for it, your very thought of *I'd like to do that* comes out of an intuitive awareness of the potential of inner growth possibility that's always within you. You don't get it out here, you have it within you already.

All you have to do out here is provide or get involved in an environment that encourages it, and releases it, and nurtures it. So that little seed, that little spark of life within you, begins to unfold, but it's always within you. It is always you. It's a reality even before you work for it. It's the whole of you, which you at this point are expressing only in part.

It is that of you that is always whole, even if the surface self is ill, or confused, or in poverty. There is always something in you that is whole. That's why I say the fundamental key to spiritual healing is that there is an Allness even within your illness. The illness suppresses the potential for Allness, but the Allness is the key.

The idea of overcoming illness is not a matter of getting treatment to do something from the outside, to change, to alter something that I previously was not before. I can be healed because I am whole. There's no other explanation. I can be healed because I'm whole. I can do more because I am more, because that's the reality of me.

Paul challenges us to "Stir up the gift of God within" (2 Timothy 1:6). He seems to mean that we can awaken the sleeping giant of our God Self at any time, and find power, or healing, or guidance, to meet any need. We probably do this occasionally. By just believing in the power within to do what needs to be done, we often exceed ourselves and excel our past performances, and we say, "Well, I guess I'm better than I thought I was." We indicate that we have certain ingenuity and creativity. It's nice to know that one can do better from time to time, but occasionally, we may do something that defies reason.

You've had those experiences, and I have. I hesitate to even talk about them, but we all have them, where in some act of spontaneous faith or some mystic moment of illumined consciousness, something happens. We do what we unblushingly refer to as the impossible, and sometimes, as I say, you don't even want to tell people about it because you can't explain it.

These things are often called *miracles* for want of any rational explanation, but that which God has done, God can do, and that which you have ever done, you can do.

## GOD DOESN'T INTERVENE

There's no way to justify a phenomenon such as that which was recorded in *Time* magazine a number of years ago.

It's a story of a woman in Florida, convalescing after a long, serious illness. She was sitting in her wheelchair; she hadn't been on her feet for months. She was emaciated and with hardly the strength to handle herself, but there she sat. She was home alone, her husband was away, with the exception of her young son, who was working out in the front yard on his old jalopy. He had the wheels off, and he had it up on blocks, and he was working underneath it doing something. Suddenly the mother watched, shocked, as the car lurched and fell, crushing the son. The whole life of the boy was about to be crushed out, and he was screaming for help.

So here was the invalid mother who lived on a farm, a long way away from the nearest neighbor. Her husband was away. There was no way to get any help—nothing there but her. So she leaped to her feet, ran to the car, braced herself, picked up the car by holding on to the bumper, lifted the car off the boy, and he got out. She collapsed.

This was recorded in *Time* magazine. The doctor was dutifully called eventually. He gave her a thorough examination, and he remarked that it was amazing that she wasn't more damaged. She had ruptured her back, some of the muscles and so forth, but finally after he heard the whole story, and he had no way except to accept what had happened, he finally said, and this was recorded also in the *Time* magazine story, "I just wonder how far she might have been able to lift that car if she'd been well."

In greater or lesser ways, we've seen that kind of thing happen in our own lives. Usually we chalk it up as just one of those things, or a miracle, or something or other, or the intervention of God, but God doesn't intervene. This is where we make a mistake. We deal with life out of our sense of inadequacy, saying, "Well, I guess God found me," or "God looked with favor upon me," or "God came out of the blue and helped me." God doesn't come out of the blue! God is the Allness potential that is always present. We either suppress it or release it.

Out of our sense of inadequacy, we say, "Well, God did it." As in God took away the life or God gave the life. Don't blame God and don't give the credit to God except for the God activity that is manifesting in and through you. Give yourself a pat on the back, not from the ego sense but from the realization of getting rightly centered in the process as it works.

God can do no more for you than he can do through you, through your consciousness, through your faith, through your understanding. It's important to keep that context always. The key to this experience is the ever-present potentiality, the mystic act of faith that releases the process, and a power, and a uniqueness, and an I AM-age that is always present.

Wouldn't it be wonderful if we could know that? If we could really live in that consciousness, we could all be superhuman. Fact is, we can all at least be a little more super in terms of exceeding our past performance in all the things we do. American author Elbert Hubbard used to say, "Man's not what he thinks he is, but what he thinks, he is."

## WHO DO YOU THINK YOU ARE?

Life is forever asking you and me, "Who do you think you are?" When the boss comes in and lays a task on your desk that is impossible for you to achieve in the time that he wants it to be done, in a sense, the task is saying to you, "Who do you think you are?" Quite often we fall short at that time. We say, *Well, I'm only human. What does he expect of me?* Who do you think you are? The only real answer is, "I AM."

If you want to carry it to its full completion, "I AM the Christ, the son of the living God." What does he think I am, perfect? I don't care what he thinks I am. The important thing is how do I think I am? If I realize that perfection is a potential within me—not that I'm perfect in manifestation, I'm perfect in potential but I'm not perfected—this is an opportunity to grow. Instead of resisting it, fighting it, let me say, "I am the God Self expressing as me and I can do what I need to do." I touch that button and I begin to release potentialities that have never been expressed before, and suddenly I find that the work just does itself.

It just does itself when I get out of the way, when I stop resisting, when I let go of that tendency to suppress the potentialities that were always present.

This is true of any relationship. When you run into somebody on the street, if somebody fights you for a seat in the subway, life itself is asking you, "Who do you think you are?" What is your answer? Quite often we come up short. We're too busy talking about that so-and-so or berating ourselves for getting into such a circumstance, but who do you think you are? "I AM the Christ, the son of the living God. I have the power, the capacity, to be nonresistant, to do what needs to be done, to brush myself off, and to move on."

Walk on. Who do you think you are? You may appear to be sick, but your sickness is only a partial expression, a frustration of the whole of you. You may be poor, you may be out of work, but this doesn't really represent the divine potential of you.

What are you? You are what you can be, and what can you be? You have to decide that. God has created you in his image and likeness, so you can be what you need to be at any time, whatever the experience is. You have the capacity to deal with it, to rise above it, to be blessed by it, and to go on.

You are what you can be, and what can you be? A perfect, healthy, radiant expression of the living God. You can be the I AM-ness fulfilled.

This is not, however, easy to see in ourselves. We're not accustomed to seeing it in ourselves. We're accustomed to looking in a mirror, and as one woman once told me, "Every time I go by a mirror, I look in it and I go, 'Eh.'" We're accustomed to thinking of ourselves out of inferiority, out of self-disrespect, out of a vindication of the problems and limitations of life, or the idea, *Well, it's nice if some people have potentialities, but I don't have them.* Some people jokingly say, "I must have been behind the door when God passed out the brains." All these ridiculous self-judgments that we make of ourselves.

We need to build up a new awareness or begin to see ourselves, as Paul says, "Not in a mirror darkly, but face-to-face" (1 Corinthians 13:12). See ourselves as the I AM-age of the divine process. You have a God potential within you and you have to respond, and every time life presents you with a challenge of any kind, shape, or form, life is asking you, "Who do you think you are?" How do you respond? "I AM." "I AM the Christ, the son of the living God. I have the capacity to deal with this, and I know that I'll get through it. I'm going to do it. I will do it easily and I will do it well." I know that the result is not placed through somebody else, but simply an acknowledgement in myself that

I am achieving the divine potential that has been mine from the beginning. When we begin to deal with life on that basis, life takes on new meaning.

## MIRROR FEEDBACK TECHNIQUE

I'm going to suggest, as a homework assignment, that you think about this. I'm going to suggest that you use the mirror feedback technique in your imaging consciousness. Literally and figuratively, occasionally stand before the mirror and look at yourself, without sticking out your tongue, and ask yourself, "Who do you think you are?" Not whimsically, but seriously, *"Who do you think you are?"*

Ask yourself this, remembering that you are not simply flesh, that you're not simply environed by a hostile environment, that you're not simply a person who's in this experience of life at the mercy of the whim and circumstance of the change in human events, but you are an individualized expression of the divine process expressing as you.

Do you see tremendous potentialities for release and growth? Who do you think you are? I AM. I AM, and I am divine potentiality expressing as me. I AM the Christ, the son of the living God. I would like you to—when you stand in front of a mirror—go through this exercise. See yourself. Carefully look beyond the appearance and say, "I AM the Christ, the son of the living God," figuratively in a time of meditation, or sitting at your desk at the office, or wherever else you find yourself feeling surrounded by hostile experiences. Just close your eyes for a moment, look into a figurative mirror, and say, "Who do you think you are?" Then respond, "I AM. I AM one. I AM whole. I AM the eachness within the Allness of God. I AM an individualized expression of a divine potentiality that is limitless. I AM the Christ, the son of the living God." That can be a healing treatment, but it can also redirect our whole attitude toward ourselves and toward life.

## ELLA WHEELER WILCOX POEM

Let me close with a poem by Ella Wheeler Wilcox. This is one of my favorites. She says:

The Creed

Whoever was begotten by pure love,
And came desired and welcome into life,
Is of immaculate conception. He
Whose heart is full of tenderness and truth,
Who loves mankind more than he loves himself,
And cannot find room in his heart for hate,
May be another Christ. We all may be
The Saviors of the world if we believe
In the divinity which dwells in us
And worship it, and nail our grosser selves,
Our tempers, greeds, and our unworthy aims,
Upon the cross. Who giveth love to all;
Pays kindness for unkindness, smiles for frowns;
And lends new courage to each fainting heart,

And strengthens hope and scatters joy abroad—
He, too, is a Redeemer, Son of God.

—Ella Wheeler Wilcox

## Meditation

*I want you to be still with me for a moment. I would like you just to whisper for yourself right now, "I exist. I exist." Right here and right now, the whole universe is projecting itself in focus through an infinite and wonderful idea, which I AM. This is God's image and likeness. Whatever else I am, it is simply this I AM-ness that is being suppressed, seeing in a mirror darkly.*

*Let me remember and never forget that beyond the appearance, beyond the human, beyond the flesh, beyond the limitations of relationship and environment, there's an Allness. There's a wholeness. There's an I AM-ness. This is what I really am. When life asks of you, "Who do you think you are?" there's really only one answer, and it comes easily. I AM. I AM whole. I AM an individualized expression of the Infinite. I AM the Christ, the son of the living God.*

*May you go forth this day, conscious of this great depth, committing yourself to the practice of it, dedicated to the realization that you are created in God's image and likeness. The image of God is the reality of you at the center of you. It is the wholeness of you that is present even if you're experiencing in part.*

*Asian cultures have an expression, Namaskar. It's spelled N-A-M-A-S-K-A-R and pronounced Na-ma-SKAR. It strictly means,*

*"The divinity within me salutes the divinity within you." It's a beautiful realization to hold and use to get centered in your awareness of the truth about other persons, but it's so especially good in helping yourself when you look in the mirror. Just whisper to yourself, "Namaskar." That's all. The first thing in the morning when you stand before the mirror, perhaps to shave, or to wash, or to dress, just quietly say, "Namaskar." I salute the divinity within you. I see you as God's perfect child. Perfect in potential, yet not perfected. Lots of work to do. Perfect as a potential creature for expression. Namaskar.*

# 3

## THE ART OF THINKING

### INCIDENTS DO NOT CAUSE THOUGHTS

THE STUDY OF metaphysics gives us a new perspective for dealing with the world. In a very real sense, it introduces us to a new dimension of reality. When we first get into the study of metaphysics, there's a tendency to get on our charger like Don Quixote and go out and try to change the world. But one of the fundamentals that often is overlooked is that metaphysics does not deal with changing the world. The whole principle is based upon ourselves. It is not the world that we're concerned about, but our thought about the world.

The important key to effective living then is not trying to find the way to set things right, to straighten people out, and to get the world to stop acting like it does. I've often taught not to set things right but to see them rightly. Right seeing is the fundamental essence of Truth. Metaphysics is a technique in right seeing, helping you to see things from a particular perspective—as Ralph Waldo Emerson would say, "from the highest possible point of view." All this is wrapped up in what we're calling today the art of thinking.

It seems to me that the greatest neglect in education today is a failure in the instruction in the art of thinking. In other words, the whole thought process is often simply taken for granted. We're thinking creatures, and so we think, and we're told what to think. When we're exposed to all sorts of levels of learning, we're supposed to think about them, and to memorize them, and to report them back much as we've heard them. Yet it is rare in education that we're introduced to the process of how to think.

The mind is dealt with, for the most part, as a fact collector and a word dispenser, and this is unfortunately also true in the study of metaphysics. We're constantly building in and programming our mind with affirmations, techniques, treatments, and so forth. We learn to verbally repeat them and picture them in the words we express.

Thought, for the average person, is a reflex process. Things happen and we react in thought. We become worried, we become fearful, we become concerned and anxious, or, on the other hand, we become happy and inspired. We assume, and this assumption is almost universally prevalent among people, that the thoughts we think are produced by the circumstances we experience and the mind is something we hold within in our skull by which we can deal with the world out there. Things happen, and we react, we think, and we say, "Well, of course I'm upset. You'd be upset, too, if you had the same experiences."

Life is a continuous reaction to outside stimuli for the average person. One may be happy, or sad, or life has meaning or is meaningless by evidence of what happens to us from day to day. We may even sometimes check the weather, or consult the stock market returns, even go to a doctor to see how we feel. Ask the average person, "How do you feel today?" and that person might say, "I don't know. I have to wait until I get down to the office to see what kind of a mood the boss is in." But contrary to all this, experiences do not cause thoughts.

Someone may do something to you and may give you a perfect opportunity to be upset if you want to be upset, but if you don't want to be upset, you need not be. Incidents happen. It becomes history once it's happened, but as far as your experience is concerned, the incident is completely external. It's always on the outside. What happens in your mind happens as a result of *your* attitudes, and *your* feelings, and *your* habit patterns. Your mind is your domain.

This is fundamental and so important to get this into our consciousness. You think what you *want* to think or you think what you have habitually thought by a certain tendency of habit patterns. Your thoughts are always your reactions to the incident, but the incident did not *make* the thought. It is your mind, and you have been thinking and reacting in thought according to the level of your consciousness.

I was talking to a young man in a hotel one day, one of the hotel clerks. There were a lot of people coming in for a convention, and they were busy, and people were there early, and other people were staying late, and the usual thing that happens in hotels. He told me, "Boy, I sure have problems tonight," and I could feel sorry for him. I talked to one of the other clerks a little later and he had an entirely different thought. He said, "People sure have problems tonight." Both of them were dealing with the same experience but having different reactions. People may have problems, but *I* have problems because of the way I'm reacting to people's problems. If I keep myself in perfect peace, then I'm simply concerned that people have problems. They're on the outside and I can handle them.

When was the last time you said, "He makes me so mad," or, "That just tees me off"? Of course, this is not correct at all. No one ever makes you mad. No one ever gets you upset. As I often say, you are upset because you're upset-able. You're angry because you have an anger consciousness that when touched, like a little red button, causes it to blow up within yourself. The anger is already within, so you react according to the level of your attitudes, according to your consciousness. Some of us are completely unaware of the fact that we have the power to control the kinds of thoughts that run rampant in our minds, and we lose any sense of mental mastery.

That's the thing that's fundamental in this study of Truth: You realize that it is *your* mind. Therefore, you have to ask yourself a question from time to time when you find yourself terribly upset or concerned about something that's happened. Take a good look at yourself and ask yourself this one question. Don't ask, "Why did they do this? Why is the world falling apart? Why do we have so many problems in life?" Do ask, "Why do I allow people, or experiences, or things to determine how I'm going think, or feel, or act?" This we can do something about.

In the same way we tend to succumb to mass beliefs, to group psychology, to sublingual suggestion, we're susceptible to the programming of mass media that is designed especially to control and influence thought simply because we've allowed ourselves to react. This is why mass media is so successful. Because of these patterns of reactive thinking, we are led into a life that is not really our own. We don't live *our* lives. We live lives that are conditioned by outside stimuli, but that's because we refuse to accept our responsibility for our own thoughts.

## YOU ALWAYS HAVE A CHOICE

The first step in this process that we're calling the art of thinking is to know that no matter what happens in your world, no matter what happens out there, no matter what you read in the newspapers, no matter what is taking place around you or to you, *you always have a choice.* You don't have to be angry. You don't have to be unhappy. You don't have to be worried. You don't have to be fearful. You can choose to think positively or creatively if that's the way you want. You can become the master instead of the slave, but it's not easy. It's not easy to take possession of your mind. To change from being a reactive thinker to a creative thinker takes a lot of discipline and will and commitment, because we've been thinking in the other way so long.

It's not easy to think happiness when you're unhappy, because your unhappiness is busy manufacturing more unhappy thoughts. We're busy manufacturing negative thoughts to fill the negative state of consciousness, and it goes around and around. It's a vicious cycle. In a very real sense, it could be said that if someone asks you what your occupation is, if you want to be realistic about it, you can say, "I'm a manufacturer." I'm always manufacturing the kinds of things that happen in my life according to my consciousness. The key, of course, is to begin doing this deliberately and not unthinkingly.

There's a classic story of a woman who was sitting, commiserating about a lot of her problems. She was talking about them—almost counting them one by one like rosary beads. One of her friends tried to console her. He said, "Oh, come on now. Things are not that bad. After all, you should try to be positive." She protested, "I don't see it that way. It seems to me when the Lord sends me tribulations, it's my duty to tribulate."

Some people seem to you should be unhappy, that you should be negative. If you walk into an office someday smiling, and singing, and whistling, people say, "What do you have to be so happy about?" But as I say so often, you don't ever need anything to be happy about. You can be happy simply because you want to be happy. Abraham Lincoln once said, "A man is about as happy as he makes up his mind to be." This is the key to the positive life. This is the key to positive thinking. It's not filling your mind with a lot of happy platitudes; it's simply determining that you have control and you can think the kinds of thoughts that you want to think. It is making the commitment at the beginning of the day and regulating through the day that you're not going to allow people, or conditions, or circumstances to decide how you're going to think or feel.

I say this to a person who wants to be a good, positive, Truth student: Don't stop reading the newspaper or listening to the news unless you find that you do not have the developed capacity to keep the news on the outside. If you don't, then you better not read the news for a while until you keep yourself in perfect peace and develop the capacity to control your own thoughts. Then you can read the news, and listen to the news, and see what's going on in the world, saying that, "The world has problems today," not, "I have problems." Suddenly you're in a state of consciousness in which you can be a creative asset to the world; you're not going to be destroyed by it.

## YOU ARE A THINKING CENTER WITHIN DIVINE MIND

The great need is for a discovery of one's self as a thinking center within the infinite Mind of God. Divine Mind essentially is your *milieu*. This is important. You're in it—all of it—all the time. It is impossible that you should ever have a mind apart from Divine Mind. All you have is a consciousness within Divine Mind. Your mind is not separate from mine. Quite often people say, "Well, I'm praying so that I can get into Divine Mind." There's no way you can ever get into Divine Mind because there's no way you can ever get out of it. You're a thinking center with Divine Mind. You're a consciousness within it. The intelligence that is in back of all thought is the intelligence that runs the universe.

Of course, we direct this intelligence into the molds of our consciousness, into the molds of human awareness, like the limitless air that we force into balloons of various sizes and shapes. It's the same air, but through our selection, we fill any size and shape we wish. So this is how we direct divine intelligence.

## Distorted Thought Manifests Distortion

In the same way, we can permit the creativity of the universe to flow into a mold of twisted and distorted thought. By the same law that would manifest perfection, in accordance with a perfect mental mold, it will manifest distortion in accordance with our distorted mental state.

Now, this is an important realization. There's only one basic intelligence, which we distort and pervert according to where we are in consciousness. We're creatures of habit who tend to habitually blow air into certain balloons simply because that's what we've always done. We have a tendency to think of ourselves as being too old or perhaps too young. We think of ourselves in certain habit patterns of sickness, of poverty, of war, and all the various things besetting human consciousness. These are the habit patterns of human mind. Quite often we think of it in terms of bad luck, and it's important to understand that what we call "bad luck" is simply a bad mental habit.

People often say, "Well, things like that always happen to me. What are you going to do?" Well, you can always *do* something. You might not be able to immediately change the conditions, but you can change what you do about them, how you react to them, and what you think about them. You can always be creative. You can always be positive regardless of conditions. In other words, tune yourself into an entirely different dimension.

It's a good thing, I think, to occasionally take inventory in our lives and to look for the situations that tend to repeat themselves—problems that repetitiously keep manifesting in our work, in our finances, in our health, in our relationships. Are you a person who keeps catching colds, or a person who keeps coming against financial difficulties, or is always losing a job?

You may not be able to change the things in the office. You may not be able to change the things in the world, but you can change the way you deal with them, which makes all the difference in the world. If you don't believe this, take a look at this simple illustration of the sailing boat. Remember that poem by Ella Wheeler Wilcox in which she says, "Some ships drive east, and some drive west by the self-same winds that blow. 'Tis the set of the sails and not the gales that determine the way they go." A ship then can move eastward and westward by setting the sails, and regardless of the one wind, so it is in your experience. Regardless of what happens by changing the way you deal with it, by the attitudes you hold toward it, you can change the whole experience as far as you're concerned.

## Taking Responsibility for Thought Changes in Your Life

It is so important to know that if you refuse to accept responsibility for your thoughts, to own your own thoughts, and you insist that these things, and conditions, and your thoughts about them are caused by the things out in the world, there's little you can do about changing them. If you're unwilling to accept responsibility for your thoughts, that's the way life is. But if you take responsibility for your thoughts, if you always recognize that whatever happens in your mind is a result of your consciousness, nobody made it happen. If you're upset, it's because you were upset-able. If you're disturbed and anxious, it's because of a level of your awareness. It's not the conditions, nor the things. If you take responsibility for them, and admit that your states of consciousness within your own mind are responsible, then and only then are you in a position to fulfill the realization that you can change your life by altering your thoughts.

You can change your life by altering your thoughts if you know that your thoughts are the problem in your life. This is something that requires a great change of the whole general perspective by which we tend to view life. Because I know that most of us tend to be defensive; we tend to be reactive. We tend to try to point the finger of responsibility at all sorts of people. Most of us have a little bit of paranoia within us. We feel that people are always picking on us or that the world is always against us. But the important realization is that you have the capacity to decide how you're going to think. You can't change people. You can't change the world, but you can change what you think about them, and then you can change your life by altering your thoughts.

## POSITIVE THINKING IS NOT JUST A PROGRAMMED MIND

There's a subtle point that is rarely observed in metaphysics. You've read articles about it, and there are books about it: You are what you think. Right? You are what you think, and I say that is totally inaccurate. You are not what you think. Now, that seems to be a matter of paradox because here we are talking metaphysics, and this is a general axiom in metaphysical studies, you are what you think. I say it's totally inaccurate. You are not what you think. You are *thinking* what you think.

This is a very important distinction because the you that thinks what you think is more than the thoughts you're thinking. The thoughts are in your mind, and you have the power to control your mind. If I am what I think, then my thoughts are me, and if my thoughts are negative, then I'm negative: *What am I going to do about it? That's just the way it is. I'm just a negative person. I was born that way. My parents have been that way. That's the way I grew up,* you see? But it is simply not true. I am *not* what I think. I think what I think, and I have the capacity to think whatever I decide to think, if I realize I have that ability and begin to exercise that prerogative.

You are not just a mind that thinks. You are a unique and wonderful identity with an Infinite Mind, and you have the power to think what you want to think and to react as you train yourself to react. Now, this is important. It's not a simple thing. We're expressing it in a very simple way, but it's a fundamental truth that is important.

The idea that if you "think certain positive things, you're going to have certain positive conditions in your life" has changed a great deal of the general thoughts and feelings of people in the world. It is positive thinking and I'm sure it's had a great influence. But let me say this: Positive thinking is not sitting around holding thoughts, filling the mind with platitudes and self-motivating images. This, you see, is not essentially positive thought at all.

# POSITIVE THINKING IS BEING ATTUNED TO YOUR POTENTIAL

Positive thought is a matter of tuning yourself into the infinite positive, which is the creative process that always flows within you.

In metaphysical teaching, there's a lot of emphasis on building things into the subconscious mind. Quite often it's said, "Now, if you take these tools and build them into your mind, program your mind with these positives, then you're going to have a creative and fulfilling life." But this is not exactly fulfilling the spiritual process. You do not ever need to build tools into your subconscious mind. Now, again, this goes against the grain of a lot of things you've heard in old-school metaphysics. You *don't* have to program tools into your subconscious mind because the truth is already the essence of Infinite Mind, and you are the creative expression of Infinite Mind. You are an identity within it. So the key is not to fill up the mind with metaphysics, but to *wake up* the consciousness to the fundamental level of your nature, which is already fundamental truth.

You *are* a spiritual being. This is why we say that there's no point in trying to be more spiritual. You can never be any more spiritual than you already are because you are a creative creature, a spiritual being, formed in the identity of the infinite process within you. This is what you really are. You can't change this but you can change your awareness of it. You can wake up to it. So it's not building it into your mind to keep saying the thing over and over and over to yourself, because it's like the person who says, "I'm not afraid. I'm not afraid. I'm not afraid. I'm not afraid. I'm not afraid. I'm not afraid." What this person is really saying is, "I'm scared to death."

Metaphysical thinking is not programming the mind with positives. It's waking up the mind to the deep underlying positive, which is the Truth of your being. You are the creative expression of this infinite process. When you think of yourself as being capable and creative, you are not going to make yourself capable and creative. You cannot say to yourself over and over, "I'm a creative creature. I'm a creative creature. I'm a creative creature. I do creative things beautifully, wonderfully all the time." You're not going to become creative because you keep saying that to yourself.

You're not going to be creative because you say you're creative, but when you understand the technique involved, you say you're creative because you know that innately you are creative. It's very subtle, but it's very important.

This is the little bone I have to pick with the so-called self-image psychology. You can program your mind with a whole new image. Plaster it over your subconscious mind with a whole new image of yourself and a whole new way of seeing yourself, but behind it all is the same scared little person you've always been. You simply act differently. You simply put on the façade, but underlying it all is the same person because you really believe you are uncreative. When you think of yourself as being capable, you don't fake "capable." You simply let the light shine through your innate potential.

A teacher uses this example: "When the weathervane points to the north, it does not make the north wind blow, but it simply registers the fact that the north wind is already blowing." Now, isn't that beautiful? It's a very important thing. You don't make it happen because you say it, but you say it because that's what is true. This is a fundamental aspect of Truth, the fundamental understanding of what affirmations are. Say what you believe and you'll believe what you say. You'll begin to express in a whole different way. Positive thinking does not make creative power, and it doesn't change God or conditions. Positive thinking simply attunes you to the power that is and can never change, can never be altered. You become one with this mental power, and it shines through you. Positive thinking, creative thinking, is thought that essentially is in tune with the Infinite.

American author Maxwell Maltz has referred to the mind as a "server mechanism," and a lot of metaphysical studies place a great deal of emphasis on this, thinking of the mind as a giant computer that will work for us if we program it with the right data. I say this has been a disservice to us. This takes your mind out of the context of the whole of mind. However, your mind is not separate from Infinite Mind. It is *not* if you can get some of the positives of Infinite Mind into your mind, then you're going to be a creative person. You are *already and can never be less than* an identity within Infinite Mind. This is what you always are, a state of consciousness within that. While you can change your consciousness, your consciousness may limit and obstruct in the same way that it may expand and creatively express, but it's for you to do the changing.

## WORKING WITH MIND FROM WITHIN

We want to understand this distinction between working with mind from without and working with mind from within as an intuitive flow to be released. Paul talks about this when he makes this clear distinction: "Don't let the world around you mold your life from without, but let God remold your mind from within" (Romans 12:2). Don't think of your mind as a fact collector. Don't think of the process of Truth, of trying to get it into your consciousness. Quite often people say, "I've read this book." People tell me this all the time, "I've read your book, and I've read it three or four times, and I'm certainly trying to get it into my consciousness." Save the effort. Don't try to get it into your consciousness. The book is not putting thoughts in your mind, but if it's going to be important at all, it's going to be little spark plugs that are igniting within you the awareness of that which you've already believed.

When you read something and say, "Hey, that's great," you underline it. We underline it with the subtle thought that, *Somehow I want to try to remember that. I want to get it into my mind*. The fact that you underline it is because you already remember it with a remembrance that precedes the writing of the book. You remember it because you've woken up to a consciousness within yourself that knows that is true. So say "yes" to it. Don't try to get it into your mind, but know that your recognition of it is a release of the positive power that is already flowing forth out of your mind. Not filling up, but waking up. That's a very important insight, and one that we can so easily forget.

## HORIZONTAL THINKING AND VERTICAL THINKING

I want to make the distinction here between *horizontal* and *vertical* thought. One deals with information, the other with inspiration. One deals with things as *they* are. The other one deals with things as *you* are. Get the difference? In one case, you're looking at the thing, and you see it and you say, "Well, that's the way it is. What are you going to do?" The other case is, "I see it. I recognize it. The people have problems, but I have the capacity to deal with them." Jesus said, "In the world you have tribulation, but behold, I have overcome the world" (John 16:33). I can decide how I'm going to deal with it. See, this is vertical thought.

The horizontal thought is a thought that reads the newspaper and sees the things in the world, and says, "Oh, boy. What a terrible day. Everything's wrong today. The world is falling apart." The vertical thinker sees these things, but instead of simply reacting to them, thinks the kinds of thoughts that he wants to think. Essentially, as a positive thinker he thinks the kinds of thoughts that he wants to see manifest in his life, so he becomes solution-oriented instead of problem-oriented.

Some people don't like it when I say this, but it's a very important thing to understand in terms of the art of thinking: If you're always reacting to how terrible things are—"Oh, the murders, the crime, the politicians!"—then you are in consciousness a part of society's problem, because that same negativity goes around and round. It can never stop by itself until someone demands, "Stop the ride. I want to get off." Someone gets off by saying, "These conditions are there, but I have the power to see them in a positive way, and I have the power to get in tune with a higher dimension." As Henry David Thoreau would say, "to march to the tune of a different drummer." And in this consciousness I can begin to inject into the general media of world affairs a new positive attitude. I can become part of a solution. There will be no solutions in society until we begin to think vertically about the things that happened. Make that distinction.

Think about it yourself, the matter of being a horizontal thinker or a vertical thinker. The vertical thinker doesn't close his eyes and say it doesn't happen. As Jesus said, "in the world, but not of it." I'm in the world. I read the newspaper. I know what's going on, but I also know that I am the center of my world. I know what's going on in me is positive and creative. I know I have the capacity to keep myself in perfect peace, and beyond that, to be part of the solution to the world's problems. That's the only way things are going to change in society.

## EVEN JESUS HAD NEGATIVE THOUGHTS

The positive person is not a person who never has a negative thought. This is important because quite often we tend to make it too hard for ourselves. We say, "Oh, I wanted to think positive today, but now I've found myself thinking negative thoughts. I guess that's just the kind of person I am ..." Even Jesus had negative thoughts, and he related to them frankly and openly.

When he went out into the wilderness to spend that 40-day period of fasting, he had a lot of negative thoughts. The negative thoughts are symbolized by Satan or the devil in the wilderness. Now, we've allowed ourselves to justify the whole theological process by thinking of the devil as the character with the red coat, pitchfork, horned tail, and fire coming out of his mouth, but that is just a symbol. Satan is always a symbol of humankind's limited consciousness. Something was coming to the surface in Jesus' wilderness experience, or certain thought patterns were emerging in his mind.

We're told that Jesus was tempted in all parts, and yet was without "sin," which we can see as the temptation of being in the flow of negative thoughts. Satan in the wilderness experience was tempting Jesus through his own negative thoughts, his own human habit patterns of thought that were saying, *Look, why should I starve out here? I can turn these stones into bread and get all I want to eat. I can show that I have tremendous power. I can throw myself off the top of a temple and protect myself, or I can set myself up as a king and become a great master of the world around me.* All of these were the temptations running through his mind. Not terribly negative perhaps, but in terms of the goals that he had set for himself, they were negative.

The great lesson here is where you and I might have said, "Just like me to act in that way. I go out here to fast and have a spiritual retreat, and I find myself thinking all these negative materialistic thoughts. Wouldn't you know it?" That's the way many of us might've acted, but Jesus didn't identify with the patterns. He recognized that something had to be done and decided to do it. He said, "Get thee behind me. Get thee hence." In other words, he said, "No." This is a tremendous lesson we cannot overlook (Matthew 4:1-11).

## YOU CAN SAY 'NO' TO NEGATIVE THOUGHTS

It's as simple as watching television and deciding that you don't like a program. Do you just sit and watch it?

This is like the classic comment from a letter to the editor. A woman said, "I think it is terrible, the awful fare on television, that me and my family have to sit and watch every night." The editor responded in a little cryptic note, "What about the off switch?" That's the thing we overlook. You can say "No!" The thought patterns are in your mind, and you're in control. The fact that you have a negative thought doesn't mean that you're a bad person, but are you going to let all that negative thought take possession over you or are you not going to identify with it? You have the capacity to say "no," to turn it off. When there's a symptom that indicates you're moving into the clutches of illness or financial depression, say "no" to it.

For instance, a classic illustration is the person who sneezes. *Ah-choo! Oh, I guess I'm catching a cold*. Why the negative thought? *Ah-choo! I've caught a cleansing*. Why not turn it around? Why not say the sneeze is getting rid of the impurities, and therefore, I'm well? As a matter of fact, it's probably more physically true because the sneezing gets rid of germs, so let them go. *I've caught a cleansing. Praise, God, I'm free*! Instead of allowing yourself to feel, *Oh, it's terrible. It's terrible. This virus is going around. I guess I'm getting it.* No. Turn it off. Turn to another channel. Get yourself into a different wavelength.

When we understand the way a mind works, we begin to realize we have the capacity to turn from one level of thinking to another. It's your mind, and you can think what you want to think. You don't have to follow along the old habit patterns, the old habit tracks of negative thinking. You can think in another way. As Jesus said, "Get thee behind me, Satan." "I refuse to go along with this anymore. I'm a spiritual being, and I know that my life is constantly in the flow of Spirit. I give thanks for the renewing process that's taking place within me right now and always."

You can reverse thought habits at any moment by simply refusing to identify with them. Stand aloof from your difficulty, from your thought, or your average thoughts that you have about them, and just say, "No. I refuse. I let it go." It's like the story of the little girl who was riding her bicycle around the neighborhood. She sat in front of a family friend's house after she fell and skinned her knee. She obviously hurt herself pretty badly, so she's sitting on the curb, and she's rubbing her knee stoically. A man came up, and he was concerned. He said, "Oh, darling. Are you okay?" She says, "Yeah, I'm all right." "Doesn't it hurt?" he said. She said, "Yeah, it hurts." "Why don't you cry?" he said. She said, "I just say to myself, 'Stop that,' and make myself mind me." Out of the mouths of babes. There's a young girl who is already beginning to realize she has power and control over her thoughts. She can think the kinds of thoughts she wants to manifest in her life.

Not that crying would have been bad, but she decides.

## What Discipline Really Is

We're simply saying that you have the capacity to make yourself mind you. This is what discipline really is. Some people say, "Well, I'm not a very disciplined person. That's just one of those problems in my life." All right. Keep right on saying it. Keep right on affirming for yourself, *I'm not disciplined. I'm not disciplined.* The fact is that we are all disciplined creatures because we *always do the kinds of things that we really want to do.* Sometimes there are certain things we don't want to do, so we allow our lack of discipline to take us in that direction. The point is: It is your mind, and you have the power to think what you want to think. Of course, it needs commitment, discipline, and at least as much attention as we give to food or bodily appearance.

For instance, how many of us, at the beginning of the day, stand before a mirror and care for ourselves physically with meticulous detail? If we're a man we shave, or if we're a woman we do our hair, we put on our eye make-up, and we take care of our nails. We select and arrange our clothes, fix our tie, and we preen before the mirror for a good while before we're ready to go out in the world. This is fine. There's a certain self-image involved in this that's important. But what about our state of mind?

We're getting ourselves all ready to face the world properly attired and acquitted and so forth. But how are we going to face the world in terms of our mental consciousness? Are we ready to face the world with our mind positive, at peace, and in tune with the divine flow, or do we just simply go out and say, "Well, I wonder what's going to happen today?"

It sounds like the story of the airline pilot who carefully grooms himself for the flight. He gets his knowledge of all the instruments, makes sure they're all carefully working, and then he taxis the plane down the runway. He gets it up into the air and he fulfills his job as a skillful pilot. He lets go of the controls, and he turns to the copilot and says, "Well, I wonder where the plane's going to take us today?" Unconsciously, this is the kind of attitude with which so many of us face life. We may be all ready for the day physically, we have our personality all out in front of us, but mentally, we don't know what's going to happen. We've become totally submissive to any vagrant, negative thought that flows into our mind.

## THE IMPORTANCE OF MENTAL PREPARATION

What advantage is it to face life meticulously outfitted if one is mentally disheveled?

This is something we have to think about. It's more important to prepare yourself mentally for the day than it is physically. It probably feels nice to be physically secure, trim, neat, and so forth, but it's much more important in terms of your contribution to yourself and to the world that you are mentally prepared for the day—important to get yourself in tune with the divine flow. It's like a runner getting ready for a race, stripping off the unnecessary attire, and then letting go of the habits that bind the mind.

For instance, if you labor under an inferiority complex, how often do you awaken in the morning and begin immediately to harp on the same old tune? *I have an inferiority complex. That's just the way I am. In fact, I was born with it. It's tattooed on my forehead: Inferiority Complex.* We start our day still harping on all the attitudes and feelings relative to this, so we tend to think of ourselves as an inferior person, which isn't true.

I don't care what kind of a complex you have. I don't care how deep-seated your inferiority complex is, you're not an inferior person. You are a person with inferior thoughts, and that's the difference. When you understand your inferior thoughts, you can change those thoughts. You can begin to do it today.

A person may have a failure complex, and tend to think of himself as a failure, but you're not a failure. I don't care how many times you have failed, you're not a failure. Just think of the researcher who fails time and time and time again, but he's not a failure because he's a researcher. He profits by every failure. You're not a failure, and you are a child of God. You are in infinite identity with an Infinite Mind, and you have the capacity to think the kinds of thoughts you want to think. You can change the failure complex. You can change the inferiority complex. You can change the sickness complex. You can change any kind of complex by determining that these are things that are going on within you, but you're in control. You're in charge, and you have the responsibility, and the opportunity, and the privilege of altering your thoughts—thus changing your whole life.

You see, you are not what you think. You are thinking what you think. Let's be very clear about that. You are not what you think. You are thinking what you think. I'd like you to get that thought so clearly in mind that it just rings a bell every time you think of it. Maybe you'd like to say, "I'm not what I think. I'm thinking what I think." Let's whisper that together: "I'm not what I think. I'm thinking what I think."

Remember that. Make a note of it. Write it on a piece of paper and put it on your desk so that you think about it. The "I" that thinks has the capacity to think what it wants to think, and I decide to think positively and creatively, and I can do so. You can be as happy as you make up your mind to be. You can be as successful as you let yourself be. You can be as healthy as you expect yourself to be.

# MAKE UP YOUR BED AND MAKE UP YOUR MIND

I want to give you a little homework assignment. It came to me a number of years ago when I was listening to the radio. I was listening to a radio interview with Robert Frost, the great poet. Someone was asking him to try to explain his tremendous, contagious optimism. "How can you always be so positive and optimistic? How can you always be so happy? What's the key? What's the secret to the success of your attitude?"

Frost said, "It seems to me the important thing for creative and positive living is man's capacity to mold and shape things." People have the power to mold and shape, thinking in terms of being a manufacturer. You can shape things as you will. He said, "I've decided long since that whenever I face the day, after I wake up, before I go down and listen to the radio, or read the newspaper, or face my wife, or go out into the world, I do two things before anything else: The first thing I do is to make up my bed, and the second thing is to make up my mind.

"The reason for the first is that it's physical. It's something I can actually do, so I physically make up the bed. Straightening up the covers and rolling the sheets and the wrinkles of the bed. But while I'm doing this I get the feeling of identification with my mind, that I'm making up my mind. I'm getting the wrinkles out of my mind. I'm getting myself organized and orderly. I'm beginning to think the kinds of thoughts that I want to think. I make up my bed, then I make up my mind, then I go down and face the world, and I'm secure that no matter what happens, I can be on top of it."

I want us to use that as an exercise this week. When you wake up in the morning, any morning, even if your partner always makes up the bed, you say, "No. Wait a minute. I'm going to make up the bed this week." Take a few minutes before you do anything else to make up the bed. Pull the covers up, straighten it all out, get the wrinkles out, and get that sense of identification that while you're doing this, you're getting your mind in order. You're getting yourself in tune to make that sort of identification. You're getting yourself constantly identified with the individualization that you are of Infinite Mind. You live in Divine Mind, the Allness of Infinite Mind. All the creative intelligence of the universe, you live in it. It's here, and you can shape and mold it any way you wish. As you begin to shape your bed into a nice, orderly arrangement, in the same sense, you're shaping your mind into that which is positive, creative, and self-fulfilling.

If you do this simple little exercise, which perhaps is not prayer—but yet in a very real sense is probably more prayer than some of the prayers we utter—you will find that you will become more positive, more capable, and more ready to meet the experiences of the day with positive, creative power.

## MEDITATION

*Now, let's take just a minute to be still and remind ourselves that we live in the medium of Infinite Mind. The same intelligence that creates the universe is the intelligence that is the essence within every thought of your mind. Every thought of your mind is an expression of infinite intelligence—even the negative thoughts. We realize that thoughts are forced into the molds of human consciousness according* to our will or according to our interest. We commit ourselves to thinking the kinds of thoughts that we want to think, the kinds of thoughts that we want to see manifest in our lives, knowing that thoughts produce conditions.

*We affirm for ourselves:* I am not what I think, but I am thinking what I think, and the self of me that thinks has the capacity to think positively. *I decide right now that during the week to come, I'm going to think the kinds of thoughts I want to see manifest. I'm not going to react to conditions. I'm going to creatively express the positive power of Infinite Mind. I'm not going to simply be a horizontal thinker, responding and reacting to all the things that are happening in the world. I'm going to be a vertical thinker. I'm going to know that even though it would appear that there are a lot of problems out there, I don't have those problems. People have the problems. The world has the problems. I have the capacity to deal with those problems in a positive way.*

Let's make a commitment that this week we're going to discipline ourselves to keep ourselves in constant control of our minds. We're not going to be disturbed or upset if a negative thought flits into our mind because we're thinkers, and thought habits are deep-seated. We're going to know that regardless of the negative thoughts that come into our minds, we cannot identify with them. Instead of saying, "Just like me. That's the way I am. There's no hope," we can say, "I have the power and the capacity to rise above this, and I say to this condition, completely not identifying with it, 'Get thee behind me. Get thee hence.' I say, 'No!'" Then I begin to say "yes" to a lot of wonderful things, positive things. Things that I read, things that I see, things that are beautiful around me, I say "yes" to them, and say "no" to the things that I don't want to be part of my life.

# 4

---

# THE SPOKEN WORD

## LIFE AND DEATH ARE IN THE POWER OF THE TONGUE

ONE OF THE most remarkable statements of the entire Bible is, "Life and death are in the power of the tongue" (Proverbs 18:21). This is an especially startling idea because most of us, if we're really honest with ourselves, have given very little thought or attention to our words. We've simply taken speech for granted. We learn to speak, for the most part, through no conscious effort. By the time we're old enough to understand these strange, powerful, and wonderful noises that we call speech, it has become simply reflex behavior, such as eating or chewing or breathing or coughing. We just talk. What is there to say about it? You just say what you want to say.

It hardly occurs to us that there is anything about speech to be understood. We talk a lot about the art of conversation in which it is considered to be good manners for a social situation. The person keeps up a perpetual babble of nothings without giving any serious thought to what he or she is talking about or whether the words uttered have anything constructive or creative to add to the world or to the situation.

In the United States we have seen a great swing all the way from fad to serious preoccupation concerning dieting. But a watchword has been the nutritionist's axiom, "You are what you eat." Certainly, whatever we put into our bodies has a tremendous influence on our health and well-being. I'm sure many of us are giving much more serious thought to that than we previously did.

The student of metaphysics comes very quickly to agree with Jesus and his rather startling words, "Not that which enters into the mouth defiles the man, but that which comes out of the mouth" (Matthew 15:11). In other words, what comes out of your mouth is more important than what goes in. At first this seems to go against the grain of the diet faddist, but it really doesn't at all. It's an added thing. It's a supplementary consciousness, something that is equally important. We might better engage in a diet or a fast from negative words. That's probably a little more difficult than a fast from carbohydrates and sweets!

## EVERY IDLE WORD GIVES ACCOUNT IN THE DAY OF JUDGMENT

Jesus also said, "And I say unto you that every idle word that men shall speak, they shall give account thereof on the day of judgment. For by your words you shall be justified, and by your words you shall be condemned" (Matthew 12:36). This, of course, has been misunderstood because we've had this old idea that the day of judgment refers to the time when the roll is called up yonder and you'll come up before God and he looks in the big black book and says, "Well, now you said some terrible things down there." This isn't it at all. We are not talking about a point in time. The day of judgment refers to a point of reckoning, the reckoning process of the law. The day of judgment is constant because law is inexorable in its results. Every day is a day of judgment, and every day is a day of salvation. The day of judgment in terms of your words is when you pay the piper. If you make some negative statements such as, "Every time it rains, I catch my death of cold," then you catch the cold and that's the day of judgment for you. You get the results in body and affairs of the words that you have idly spoken.

## Overlooking the Matter of Speech

It's amazing that in the teaching of metaphysics there's a tendency to deal with the power of thought, the work of the subconscious mind, and self-image psychology with the imagination and feeling. These things are all very important and very helpful, yet we completely overlook this very important matter of speech: A person may deal with truths of mystic power and still allow a steady stream of negations to fall unchecked from his lips. It's much like trying to drive your car with the brakes on. You can do it, but it's not very effective, and you'll certainly burn out your brakes. And it's certainly not very good for energy efficiency either.

How often the sincere student of Truth at work on some annoying problem will be praying and treating and affirming, affirmations and words that he uses diligently and repeatedly, and he seems to feel that what he says at other times really doesn't count. He may have a statement, "I'm a child of God. I'm one with life, vitality, and Spirit now," and 10 minutes later he's saying, "Boy, I sure feel pooped." It's like saying, "King X, this really doesn't count. The only thing that counts is the positive truths that I'm muttering." But there is no King X in the verbal expression of Truth. The subconscious mind does not discriminate. Your subconscious mind cannot tell the difference between your *causal* words and your *casual* words or your *causal* thoughts and your *casual* thoughts. You may insist you were only kidding when you said, "That just burns me up," or some similar cliché, but as we say, the subconscious mind can't take a joke, and it somehow registers this consciousness, and it assumes this is a serious projection of positive power expressed in a negative way.

Jesus says we will give account in the reckoning process of law for every word, even idle words. I doubt if any of us really takes this seriously enough. We assume the only thing that really counts in terms of this power of the creative word is when we're sitting in the Silence in a quiet place, and we have our Truth books before us, and we deliberately begin to deal with metaphysical things. It is like when you leave church and go home and take off your Sunday meeting clothes, and you can get back to your normal vernacular, your four-letter words, and all the clichés that are so much a part of everyday speech. You think and assume that really doesn't count, because after all this is not really what I'm seriously involved with in metaphysics. But it really does count, at least in *practical* metaphysics, not the kind of mental metaphysics that is abstract and abstruse. Practical metaphysics means the practice of metaphysics, practicing every moment of your life. With all the words that we speak, even the idle words, Jesus said, we give account for.

# THE CREATIVE POWER OF THE SPOKEN WORD

People are creative creatures, and as we've said, the cutting edge of this creativity, the cutting edge of this whole involvement in metaphysics, is the power of the spoken word. Emerson tells us, "Man is an inlet and may become an outlet to all there is in God." *All there is in God.* More than we know, we embody the divine essence, the whole creative power of the universe, through our words, through the consciousness in which we express ourselves.

The Hebrews were taught early that, "The word is very nigh unto thee, in thy mouth, and in thy heart that thou mayst do it" (Deuteronomy 30:14). And this word, in terms of the true metaphysical aspect of this biblical teaching, is the creative *logos*. The creative logos creates us and creates through us. It is the one. It is the infinite eye. In Deuteronomy, we find the sacred crown of the Jews in the words, "Hear, O Israel; the Lord our God is one." Those of you who have a Jewish background realize that this is the ancient Shema. "Hear, O Israel; the Lord our God is one"— one God, one Lord, one power, one presence, one force, one dynamic activity. This is the fundamental unity realization that we find way back in the time of the Pythagoras. The Pythagorean system of mathematics deals with the idea that all numbers are reversible. They precede from unity and they're resolvable back into unity. They all come out of one and they're all resolvable back into one. It has been said that if we had a full knowledge of the One, of this unity, of this wholeness in the spiritual and the fundamental physical one, that we could dispense with all learning, with all mathematics, with all physics because we would have the whole all wrapped up in this consciousness of one. This is the Pythagorean system.

The same premise holds in metaphysics—all things begin with the one. The Lord our God is one. God is one presence, one power, one dynamic activity. We live in the One and we are projections out of this One, that which we call Being, Infinite Mind, God, and divine love.


## IN PRINCIPLE WAS THE CREATIVE WORD

This is the meaning of John's powerful statement. We read, "In the beginning was the word, and the word was with God, and the word was God. All things were made through him." In the original, this word was the fundamental concept of *logos*. In the beginning was the logos. To understand this, you have to realize that the word *beginning* is wrongly translated because the word is *in principio*, so the translation (which is more accurate) is "in principle." In principle, the word was God. The word. The logos. If we put this in terms of a practical realization today, we know that it says the root of your being is the creative word. You're an outlet from this fundamental, basic consciousness of oneness, which is the root of your being. So is the visible outshowing of a creative flow within you that is connected with the very root process of the universe. Your words are the outpouring of that consciousness.

# Do Not Put Into Words That Which You Do Not Want

So it becomes logical that it is simply not good sense to put into words or to formulate into verbalisms that which you really do not want to see manifest in your life.

Just stop and think a little bit about the typical conversations that pass between us and the typical expressions that come out of us in exasperation or in moments when we're off guard. The things we say, the things we put into words, things we haven't the slightest desire to see manifest in our life, but we go right on saying them anyway. It's like playing Russian roulette, and every once in a while the bullet comes into the chamber and *pow!* Then we say, "How could this happen to me? I don't deserve this!" Yet in this sense, we do.

Since we're verbal creatures, constantly involved in communication with one another, it's vitally important, as the proverb says, to "set thou a seal upon my lips," to really watch the words that come out of our mouths. This takes a lot of discipline because most of us have been totally verbally permissive. We're simply going to have to become more concerned about what comes out of our mouths.

We must be watchful that we say the kinds of things we really want to say. The things that we really want to see manifest in our life, not the kinds of things that we impetuously say out of force of habit. And these habit patterns run deep. Most of us have a long list of clichés and habit patterns of speech that we utter over and over again. If we could record our words, listening to ourselves for one day, we would be shocked if we objectively analyzed the kinds of words we were expressing in terms of the positive power of words. We would almost wonder how we could have possibly survived when the power of life and death are in the power of the tongue. Obviously, there is the grace of God involved or we would have a rough time in our lives, because we say so many negative things often in the name of being "realistic."

It's time we came to understand that true realism goes deep beneath the outward manifestation of life. If you're really going to be realistic about yourself, you're going to see yourself not by appearances, as Jesus said, but by righteous judgment. You're going to see yourself in terms of the divine potential that is within you, see yourself in terms of this divine process that is fundamental to you. If you're really going to be realistic, then look beyond the appearance, see the Truth, and do *not* be negative. Of course, it takes a lot of commitment to make that kind of change.

Now I'm not saying we should simply mouth a lot of platitudes and always have something nice and pleasant to say about everything, while refusing to recognize a fact as a fact. Obviously, we have to face up to certain needs. We have to be willing to recognize that occasionally I hurt, occasionally I need money, occasionally there's something in my life that's not working as it should work.

## LET SOMETHING GOOD BE SAID

A good rule that I use is to let something good be said. No matter what else you may be required to say, let something good be said. Let something of the God principle, something of the creative *logos*, something of the One, be articulated so that you can keep your flow and stay related and in focus with this divine process.

One of the ways you can turn your expression from negative to positive is to accept your responsibility in achieving the good you desire. For instance, if there's a lot of tension, a lot of pressure, a lot of bickering, and a lot of unproductiveness in your place of work, recognize that you are there and you're a part of it. As we say so often, you make the difference, or you can. Let it begin with you. Let the answer begin to unfold through your consciousness.

Let's be realistic, but let's also be realistic in the sense that if this is ever going to change, it has to start somewhere, and it might as well start through a change in our consciousness, in our attitude. This is true whether it's in your office or whether it's talking about the world or the crime in the city or the confusion in our neighborhoods or whatever. Let it begin with you.

## Oughtness to Isness Statements

It's like they say about politics: It's easy to throw stones. It's the *ins* against the *outs*, but when the outs get in, then the ins begin to talk about the ins that were and are now out. They're all throwing stones at one another, but nobody seems to have any positive solutions. When you're sitting in your office griping about everything, take your little notebook out and write down a series of thoughts about how you think the situation ought to unfold. How do you think it should function? How do you think people should act? How do you think workers should perform? When you say it in terms of an oughtness, then you can turn these statements around. We suggest this often as a way of creating an affirmative, positive approach. Turn the *oughtness* statements around to *isness* statements. In other words, say them as if they are actually true. Instead of saying, "This office should be a place of cooperation and mutual trust, leading to effective work and good business," you can rewrite it in terms of "divine realism." You then say, "This office is a place of cooperation and mutual trust, leading to effective work and good business."

Some would say this is Pollyanna because this isn't really what it is happening, but in denying realism, you're looking beyond the appearance and you're trying to get yourself in tune with the creative flow so you can be a part of the emerging solution, rather than remaining as a part of the problem. You're now going to be a part of the problem or a part of the solution. Which will it be? As the Bible says, "Choose ye this day whom you will serve" (Joshua 24:15), and you have to decide. But I must tell you this: If you continue to complain about it and say how awful people are and how awful the boss is and so forth, you're just as much a part of the problem as the people you think are doing all the dirty work. It's one or the other. Make up your mind. You are going to be part of the solution in a divine realistic approach, and begin to affirm the kinds of positive things that you would like to see manifest in that office. Then you'll become a part of a creative flow.

I think of that in a more personal sense, in terms of your physical condition. Instead of blurting out, as all of us are apt to do occasionally, "I feel simply terrible today," the question is, how do you think you ought to feel? As a student of practical metaphysics, you know that you ought to feel good, because you know that we're dealing with this power of creative life within us and so forth. There should be a way to release this positive power.

Quite often metaphysical students feel guilty and are even afraid to admit that they have any problems, because they know that they ought to feel good.

When you find yourself blurting out some sort of a negative, take your little notebook again and quickly write a few thoughts about how you think you ought to feel. *Well, as a spiritual being, I ought to experience health and wholeness, right?* Obviously that's the way it *ought* to be. Now rewrite that in terms of an *I AM* realization, so that you say, "I AM a spiritual being. I AM established in health and wholeness now." This is something you do within yourself.

We're dealing with the realistic appraisal of life from a metaphysical point of view. You're referring to yourself, "I AM a spiritual being. I AM established in health and wholeness now." Now you're dealing creatively with your problem rather than simply indulging in the problems. Now you're going to be solution-oriented rather than problem-oriented. See yourself in a positive light and affirm the truth for yourself: *I AM a spiritual being. I AM established in health and wholeness now.* And then not only say that as a spiritual treatment, which is one thing, but let it become so habitual that it becomes the kind of communication that is going to utter forth out of your lips in terms of the things you say about yourself and about your life. Then you're dealing creatively with your problem.

## NOT MY WORDS BUT THE WORDS OF HIM WHO SENT ME
Now let's be clear on this because it's so easy to lose what is involved. When you affirm: *I AM a spiritual being. I AM established in*

*health and wholeness now*, you're not saying this to make it true. It's not going to be true just because you say it. This is not what practical metaphysics is all about. It's not saying a lot of platitudes and if you say them long enough they're going to become real. You're actually articulating that which is true in a spiritual, realistic appraisal of life. You're getting your speech into the universal flow, and you're letting the creative *logos* be outformed in your mind and your body and your affairs.

Remember the time when Jesus was out with the disciples on the sea and there was this tremendous storm, and they awakened him in the middle of the night because they were all very fearful? They said, "Master, Master, save us, we'll perish." He looked and very quickly took appraisal of the thing, then He spoke the word of *peace*, and the winds stilled. The disciples looked at one another and said, "My God, what kind of man is this? Even the storms obey him" (Mark 4:35-41). It was called a *miracle*. To this day we put this application of a miracle upon all the things that Jesus did, such as when he spoke the word and the 5,000 people were fed. He spoke the word and people were healed—they got up and walked. The blind suddenly saw. He spoke the word of Truth and Lazarus even came forth from the dead after three days in the tomb.

Jesus gave us a key, and it's a key that is rarely uttered. It's a key that I have hardly heard mentioned, even in metaphysics, strangely enough, because it's a very dynamic and very important key that takes attention away from the thought of speaking a lot of magic words. He said, "The words I speak are not my words, but the words of Him who sent me." See what he's pointing to here? "The words I speak are not mine. Not I, Jesus, say 'Lazarus come forth.' I have gotten myself out of the way and I am allow-ing the creative logos to express through me and to be articulated in the form of my words." The ego is not involved. I'm not saying this to make it true. He didn't have to say, "Lazarus, come forth, come forth, come forth. Please come forth so I won't look like a fool before all these people." He didn't say that at all. It says he lifted up his eyes to heaven (John 11:1-44).

This is startling because we've always thought of heaven up there somewhere, but he says the kingdom of heaven doesn't come with observation; it's neither here nor there—it's within you. When he looked within, got himself in tune with the realiza-tion that he was a creative expression of infinite power, he said, "Lazarus, come forth." And the power flowed forth through his words, through his consciousness, to accomplish that whereto it was sent. This is a very vital point. I'm not saying that we should all go out and try to raise people from the dead or feed the 5,000 people or walk on water. We've got a lot more practical, mun-dane things to take care of in our own lives, in terms of getting employment, in terms of keeping our body sound and whole, in terms of getting along with our coworkers. These are vital things that can be accomplished if we know that the words we speak are not our words, but the words of him who sent us.

So often the student begins to use affirmations and metaphys-ical treatments, and they mouth them dramatically. They say, for instance, "I'm a child of God, I'm a child of God. I'm healthy and whole now," and it's almost as if they say, "Hey, I'm doing pretty good. I can really say that I'm fine." It's something we've learned, and we feel so very good about ourselves. We get this affirma-tion, this treatment, and we say it over and over again. We say it dramatically, and we say, "Oh, I'm really proud of myself. I've really learned how to say affirmations now."

## SAY WHAT YOU ARE LISTENING TO

This is not what it's all about. As a matter of fact, one of the ways we can check up on ourselves is a little cliché that I use, "Don't listen to what you're saying. Say what you're listening to." Don't listen to what you're saying. If you listen to what you're saying, you're flattering yourself because you're saying positive words. "Hey, I'm really saying some positive words. This is great. This metaphysics is real neat. If I say this over and over, something great's going to happen." However, saying what you're listening to means you must listen before you speak. We tend to speak impetuously or reflexively. We just allow the words to come forth, and we even try to learn by rote all sorts of positive statements so we can exude positive phrases instead of negative clichés. This is a step in the right direction, but this is not the key. This is not the fulfilling of the power of the positive word.

When you face any kind of a situation in which normally you would come forth with some kind of statement, negative or positive, the important thing is to listen. We need to discipline ourselves to do this. It's like the old axiom of counting to 10 before you blurt something out. Take time to turn within and to listen and see what the infinite process is saying through you. See what your body is really saying. See what your consciousness is really reflecting at the deepest possible moment, and then speak the creative logos. Remember, there's always a Divine Mind counterpart within you to anything that you experience.

Jesus says, "The Father knows what things you have need of even before you ask." I say, don't ask. Listen. Don't ask God for help. Listen. The Father knows what things you have need of, and he's already of the desire to lead you forth into the fulfillment of those things. This is a process that's already there. Listen. It's the missing link. It's the missing link in practical metaphysics.

## POWER IN THE DIVINE *LOGOS* ARTICULATED IN WORDS

We're not dealing with autoconditioning. We're not dealing with saying a lot of things to make them true. We're not dealing with any kind of metaphysical *abracadabra* magic words that accomplish great things.

Unless we understand this, we tend to feel that metaphysics is like the adult counterpart of the young person's trading baseball cards. The adults trade affirmations. "Do you have a good treatment for arthritis?" "Hey, I'll trade you my treatment for heart ailments, okay?" We trade treatments and affirmations, and we get the feeling that this little treatment, this little card that has these magic words, this can really change your life. Well, I don't want to cause anyone to be disturbed, but … maybe I do. The fact is that no statement of Truth, no word of itself, has any power in itself. Words do not have power.

Now this is startling because it goes against the grain of everything we've ever read or been taught, even some of the things that I teach. But we're saying this for a very particular effect. The words do not have power, but the words can be imbued with power if they are tuned in on the creative nonverbal word. The word is that which is nonverbal. It's the divine creative logos. Your words have power according to the attunement of the power that flows forth from within you. The affirmation doesn't have the power, so there's no point in taking this affirmation and saying it over and over as if that is going to make something happen. If you take this affirmation—and it is a very powerful device, certainly, the whole affirmative approach is a marvelous metaphysical approach to prayer—you take this prayer or treatment or affirmation, and you speak this word, but you speak it reverently and quietly in the consciousness that this is not *your* word. Then it's the word of Truth and you're tuning in on it, and you're allowing it to flow like a water faucet is flowing, and you allow the flow to manifest through you. You don't speak the word powerfully and with great effect and authority and repetitiously. Remember, Jesus said avoid vain repetitions. A certain amount of religious people have overlooked this, and a lot of metaphysical people have too. I don't care how many times you speak it. In fact, don't speak it at all. Just think it, but get yourself in tune with the creative flow, and then the word has power because it is imbued. As the scriptures would say, it's imbued from power on high. The divine process flowing through human consciousness is articulated through your words. It's a very subtle but hugely important thing.

The important thing is that the creative logos is a nonverbal process we articulate in words. You see, if the word itself had the power, and if I used a word in the English language and somebody else uses it in German, it's a different word. You say, "But it means the same thing." Well, of course, a lot of words mean the same thing. We're not dealing with the word, the logos. We're dealing with the consciousness, which we project into the words that have meaning to us. The particular phrase or statement will work for you but won't even have any effect upon someone else because you're thinking something separate and distinct and different when you use it.

All good communication comes from inner communion. There is no way that you can ever really have good communication between people except when there's a communion. It takes an acknowledgement of the one within yourself and a recognition of and a tuning in on the one within the other person, so that your communication becomes one-to-one. This is real one-to-one communication. It's from the basic one in yourself to the basic one in another. When you're in that consciousness, there will always be understanding. There will always be loving relationships. And, if you're a business person, there will always be sales. There will always be a happy, positive solution to your projections because it's one-to-one. You're tuning in to that basic One, which is the key to the creative process of the universe.

## Do Not Be Verbally Permissive

How important it is that we discipline ourselves to practice this matter of listening, readying ourselves for all communication processes? In the previous chapter, we talked about people who are very careful to ready themselves for the day by being physically outfitted and yet always remain mentally disheveled. We could add not only mentally disheveled, but also add verbally permissive. It's important that we see the need toward self-discipline and commitment to be verbally positive and creative.

We need to make a concerted effort to clean up our speech, to eliminate all the negative clichés of which we have so many, and the tendency toward self-effacement. "Oh, I always do this. I always make this mistake." Many of us have a long battery of self-effacement concepts. And we have so many pessimistic proclamations, such as, "Oh, the recession will never get over, and probably I'll be fired from my job because everybody's being laid off." We don't really want this to happen, and yet somehow in consciousness the negative seems to come out. Even though we sing songs like "Accentuate the Positive," somehow it seems the only way to be popular in conversation with people is to be the most negative of all.

## PROFANITY FRUSTRATES THE CREATIVE LOGOS

If we're really going to get serious about the power of the spoken word and about dressing up our speech, we need to learn to express ourselves without profanity. Now I'm not being moralistic. Many people say, "Well, here goes the preacher. He's gone to meddling again." We lived through a generation where people would say, "Tell it like it is. Let it all hang out." That usually means to hang out all the dirty linens you can think of, hang out all the dirty words that you can dream up—the words you learned when you were a little child. Let it all hang out, but I'm saying, and I say this very sincerely, that it's not simply a matter that four-letter words misrepresent you and indicate a lot of bad breeding. They indicate a very low-level vocabulary, and when you have a poor vocabulary, there is always poor communication.

I read something recently that's rather startling. It was a study that was made, I believe, at Harvard University relative to communication and advanced speech. They found out some rather interesting things from studies they made over a long period of time. They discovered that people who used profanity excessively—people who did not have a good vocabulary to express themselves, who are always saying, "You know what I mean?" and so forth, that these people did not have the words to really articulate what they wanted to say. They would always say, "You know what I'm trying to say, don't you?" And of course, the other person doesn't know what they're trying to say, because you're thinking one thing and they're thinking another.

They discovered that among this kind of person—and this was not simply people of underprivileged groups—was the greatest degree of violence. Because this says what the words cannot communicate. Violence will take over. If people cannot say things in words, they will use fists or clubs. This seems startling, and we might even say, "Well, that's kind of ridiculous," but this was a very serious amount of study. Then the study went on to say—and I question the total conclusions of this phase, but I'm willing to acknowledge that it's possible—that the reason for deadly violence in America as against lesser levels of violence, for instance in Great Britain, is basically because we speak such poor English. Now again these are semanticists speaking, but it's interesting. It falls in line with the very important need to dress up our speech and speaking articulately and saying things that really communicate.

If we're really trying to be positive and we're really trying to get involved in the practical metaphysical approach to life, then we need to dress up our speech, to brush up our speech mannerisms. Certainly, I believe very strongly that profanity of all kinds, along with a lot of other negations, are an effective frustration of the creative logos without which the spark necessary to happiness and health and prosperity is almost totally lacking. It's something to think about. You may take this with a grain of salt, but I throw it in as a very vital part of our lesson.

## DRESS UP YOUR WORDS

In dressing up our speech there's another aspect too. As I said, the creative logos is basically nonverbal. We articulate it in words because we are verbal creatures, but another aspect of it is to pay really close attention to the voice and to intonation. I don't mean putting on oratorical affectation, but simply so that your speech properly represents you. When Paul says, "Stir up the gift of God within you," I think it might also apply to the animation and the vitality of the voice. When you dial a number and a person says, "Hello?" in a dour tone, what kind of life does that seem to suggest? What kind of a self-image does that seem to indicate in terms of the individual? I'm not saying that one should be affected in our voice, but I think quite often we do not allow our voices to really express what we feel within ourselves.

How would you sound if you really were in the flow of life and love and power? How would you project yourself if you really did feel that you were alive, alert, joyous, and enthusiastic about life? This is something that I think we need to consider very seriously in this matter of setting a watch on our lips, stirring up the gift of God within us, and dressing up our speech. Prepare yourself for all conversation, all kinds of communication, with prayer and treatment. Listen within, identify with the inner light, and then with a glow on your face and a sparkle in your eyes and enthusiasm in your manner and tone, let something good be said. Let the positive power of the dynamic creative logos within you be projected into your words. Get the idea of communicating with people, with situations on a one-to-one basis. The One, the dynamic, the divinity within me, salutes and relates to and does business with the One, the dynamic divinity within you. Depth to depth, life to life, and in this way your words will be a part of the divine flow and will never get in the way.

You see, sometimes even metaphysical words can get in the way if the words are expressed out of a feeling of a rote learning process. I don't really understand what I'm saying, but if I say them enough something's going to happen. Sometimes the words will get in the way of our own creative flow. Get this idea of dressing up your speech and letting the positive power of the creative logos be expressed through you and all that you do. Discipline yourself to speak the creative words and say the kinds of things that you want to see manifest in your life.

## SEVEN-DAY VERBAL DIET

Now I'll give you a homework assignment, and this is not going to be an easy one. It's very simple, but it's not easy. Dieters and religious communicants quite often go on periods of fasting, so I'm going to suggest that you go on a fast. I'm going to dare you, I'm going to challenge you to go on a verbal diet for seven days. We're going to be chiefly concerned with a mental diet in terms of carefully choosing the kinds of words you express during this week. It's going to take some effort.

Challenge yourself to go on a seven-day verbal diet, where you're going to think before you speak, you're going to listen before you articulate things, and you're going to try to put into words only those things that you want to see manifest in your life. You're going to try to keep yourself from the negative clichés, from the profanity, from all the words that have no meaning whatsoever or a negative meaning, and to say only positive, creative expressions. Say them in an effective and positive way.

I've often wondered what would happen in our country if everyone would fast from negative words for one whole day. It's not hard to believe that we can go on a fast because, after all, holidays seem to attract a lot of people to go on a special fast of things that are important to that holiday festivity. We think of this in terms of one day when every single person in the population of the country would speak only when they have something important and positive to say and could express it in a creative way.

I believe that because of the articulation of the creative logos that would flow through this type of consciousness, we would begin to experience a whole new positive healing vibration in our land. I think hospitals would see patients getting well quicker. I think offices would experience an upsurge of harmony and productivity, and because of increased productivity, I would see our inflationary processes begin to reduce themselves. I would see the whole economic system of the United States right itself. I would see marvelous results, even in the interaction processes between nations in terms of peace in the world.

We're not concerned with whether it can happen out there. The important thing is, will it happen in you? You're one. Remember Edward Everett Hale, who used to say, "I'm only one, but I'm one. I can't do everything, but I can do something. But I can do what I ought to do, and what I ought to do, by the grace of God, I will do." The question is: Would you allow yourself to be a channel for positive power in terms of one week of a mental and verbal diet? We are thinking in terms of only those things that are positive and expressing them in creative and positive and meaningful ways that are important to see manifest in your life and the kinds of things you desire. The kind of world you would like to see unfold. The kinds of physical conditions you would like to have in your own body. The kinds of finances you'd like to experience. All of these things. Allow your verbal expressions to relate to and give articulation to that kind of expression in your life. Are you willing to do this? Are you willing to make an effort at it?

I can say one thing, and I can say it with sincere belief and conviction, that to any person who will work on this: You will not only become a part of the solution of a better world, a better neighborhood, a better office, but you will also find that just by the very act of your own discipline and your own participation in this positive flow, things will take place in a marvelous way in your life. You will see a change of the vibrational patterns that influence your whole life in a way that some would call miraculous. Are you willing to do it? It's very simple. Just say you're going to go on a diet. A verbal diet for seven days. Are you willing? You make the difference.

# "Let Something Good Be Said" Meditation

*Let's be still for just a moment, and let's get this whole thing back into a true spiritual context. All things begin with the basic One, the creative logos. It's not just that we like to say to ourselves that we're spiritual beings, but we like to remember at the ground of our being that each of us is Spirit being us. This is always true, whether we know it or not, whether we articulate it or not. When we listen before we express ourselves, we listen to this vibrational pattern of the universe, which is expressing itself, articulating itself as us. Dynamic, wonderful, powerful, beautiful, fulfilling, and loveful. You are a dynamic spiritual being. This is your basic identity in the universe. Make the commitment now that you're going to allow this to be the ground, the foundation, the underpinning of all that you think and feel and articulate in the seven days ahead. You're going to keep coming back to this. "All things come out of the basic one and are resolvable back into it," says the Pythagorean system, and in practical metaphysics, it's a vital realization that all positive powerful things come out of this basic One at the root of our being, and are resolvable back into it.*

*We begin with this. We listen to this consciousness before we go to work, before we face people, before we get involved in any kind of relationship, we remember who we are, and then we allow this consciousness to be embodied. As Emerson says, "Man is an inlet and may become an outlet to all there is in God." The outlet is the cutting edge of our spoken words. We project this spoken word in positive power, and the words I speak are not my words, but the words of him who sent me. I allow them to flow forth through me in faith, in creativity, in love. And let's project ourselves in imagination now, see ourselves going forth from this place, doing the normal little confrontations that we have. Let's do such things as buying subway tokens, talking to cab drivers, ordering food in a restaurant, talking to people, or conversing around the water cooler. See ourselves through mental imagination as projecting positive power, as keeping a seal on our lips, and saying only those things that are positive and creative. Say them in a loving, harmonious way, and we'll say, "Let something good be said."*

*I use the slogan LSGBS just as a remembrance. LSGBS: Let Something Good Be Said. Let it be said positively, let it be said lovingly, let it be said with animation, let it be said in a way that truly represents us in the fullest, most powerful way. In this sense, we go forth, committing ourselves to the practice of fundamental metaphysical principles in a very simple way. "And ye shall know the truth and the truth shall make you free." Amen.*

# 5

---

# FAITH

## FAITH AS BELIEF IN GOD

THE WORD *FAITH* has a tendency to be confusing, to be misleading. It creates skepticism and fanaticism, intellectual resistance, and emotional surrender. Unfortunately, faith has been considered solely a property of religion. Since we tend to think of religion as dealing primarily with Sunday worship services, faith is something we take out of the closet and dust off and put on like a Sunday suit. We talk about faith in quite a limiting way. We sing about it, preach about it, pray over it, and then with the final "Amen," it's put back into the six-day closet of unconcern.

Normally, faith seems to be the blind acceptance of a creed where you accept things on a "confession of faith." A little boy referred to it as "confusion of faith." Maybe that puts it a little more clearly, but you confess your beliefs: "I believe this," "I believe that," "I believe in the Father, the Son, and the Holy

Ghost." You remember the "I believes" of your religious background—with that you become one of the believers—and the root of the system is, "I believe in God."

## GOD BELIEVES IN ME

What does that mean?

Sidney Harris, the syndicated newspaper columnist who's a favorite of mine, once enraged the ardent believers by saying, "My father didn't believe in God, but God believed in him." Now what he meant by that was his father was not religious in the credo sense. He didn't go to church or go to synagogue. He didn't accept all the dogma and doctrines of the church, but he was a caring and sharing person. So that whatever religion purported to be, he was doing it; he wasn't professing it. He was out there doing it, living it, expressing it. God believed in him.

I often startle people in my study of prayer when I ask the question, "Do you have to believe in God in order to pray?" What a ridiculous question that may seem to be. We might say, "Of course, you do!" But, of course, I say, "No, you don't." Do you have to believe in electricity in order to turn on a light switch? You really don't. Your act presupposes a kind of belief, but it's simply a spontaneous action of doing something and the whole electrical process springs into expression for you because it can't help itself.

What I'm saying is that you don't have to believe in God in the sense of knowing all about God and having a theological position about God. If you can get in contact with the process and let it express through you by loving, not talking about love, but by loving, and by believing, then the activity of the internal process works for you. It's a very important realization to get the sense that to believe in God does not actually mean saying you believe it, doesn't actually mean going to church, doesn't actually mean professing a lot of creeds. As a matter of fact, if you believe in God out there and practice the absence of God, then you create a separation in consciousness that may well make your prayer very difficult, if not impossible. Quite often the disciples would in effect ask Jesus, "How come we can't do this?" and he would say, "You pray, but you pray amiss" (James 4:3).

## FAITH IN GOD VERSUS FAITH FROM GOD

The dynamic key is not faith *in* God, but faith *from* God. Let's think about that a little bit. Faith *in* God is trying to direct your attention consciously to something outside yourself. Faith *from* God begins with the basic premise that you live in God, you move in God, you have your being in God. God is the foundation of the ground of your being. You center yourself in that consciousness and then you believe *from* that consciousness. You're not believing in an abstraction; you're not believing in an intangible. You're believing from a consciousness, which enables you to put yourself in tune with the process.

This is a subtle thing, but I hope you can begin to get the meaning, because the Bible gives the direction, "Be still, and know that I am God" (Psalm 46:10). So then, to believe in God means to believe in yourself—to believe in yourself at the divine level, to believe in yourself as rooted in the ground in the consciousness of God. To really practice faith, first of all, you start at the ground of your being and center yourself in the consciousness of this oneness process, knowing that the whole universe is pouring itself into you, and through you, and as you. Out of that consciousness you go forth and do the things that you need to do in your life in a believing attitude. Not believing in some intangible, but projecting that faith process that enables you to have faith in yourself, have faith in people, have faith in experiences, and have faith in a divine law that is forever working so that things work together for good.

## EVERYONE HAS FAITH BUT FEW USE FAITH WELL

To really understand faith, I think we have to realize that we're dealing with something that is always present. Faith is a factor of the consciousness, and faith is just as natural to every person as seeing, as hearing, as tasting. There's really no such thing as an absence of faith. Now that may be surprising because we've talked about a "lack" of faith. Whenever a person says their problem is lack of faith, what is normally meant is having faith in the wrong things—fear is faith, worry is faith, insecurity is faith. You're simply believing in things that are negative rather than positive.

Faith is not something you're going to find somewhere. Faith is not something you're going to earn like a diploma at the end of a course of study. Faith is the free gift of God, which all people have, but only a very few people hear it rightly and with discipline. Think about that because that's so very important to understand.

# Faith Is Centering Yourself in God

There's a dynamic thought that I want you to consider, that God is centered in you. Now that's all there is to it. Just five little words: *God is centered in you.* If we could really understand that, it would change our lives. Because there's nothing you can do about this. You can't in any way get God to be centered in you more than He is now. God has already given you all that He can give you. God has created you in His image and likeness. The whole universe is centered at the point of you, and there's no way you can change it.

But we'll carry this thought a little further. You know certain people—and I do too—who have a tremendous capacity to demonstrate great things. These are the people of whom we say, "Oh, if I just had faith like that person." Or you might think of some mystic, or some healer, or perhaps think of Jesus.

The important thing is that God is no more centered in that person, or that friend, or that teacher, or that mystic, or in Jesus, than in you. God is no more centered in any great mind or great consciousness than in you. Of course, we can't stop there, because there's no denying that a person may express various levels of consciousness. When we think of someone like Jesus, obviously we realize that there's a great difference in the developed potential between Jesus and you and me. The difference is not that God is more centered in him, but that Jesus was more centered in God. This is the key: You and I are centered for the most part in things, in people, and the circumference of life. We center our attention in negation, in limitation, in a focus on all sorts of limited things.

Basically, positive faith is centering your consciousness in God, not God out there, but God in whom you live and have your being.

## THE POWER OF GOD IS ALWAYS PRESENT IN YOU

The power to do all the mighty things that we dream of doing is a clichéd type of faith. The power to do mighty things, the eternal flow of life and guidance and substance, is always in you because this is the activity of God that's centered in you. The power is always present. Substance, guidance, direction, is always present. All the love in the universe is always present in you. There's never an absence because God is presence, and presence cannot be absent. We may practice the absence because we may focus our attention on all other things except this consciousness of God. The need then is not to get God to bring Himself into our experience but for us to practice the presence instead of practicing the absence.

## FAITH IS NOT A MIRACLE CATALYST BUT A PRINCIPLE

Faith is often taught as a miracle catalyst. We're told that faith is the miracle catalyst that will make God work for you. Have you ever heard that? God will do wonderful things for you if you have faith.

God doesn't do things for you in some special way because of your faith—that's misleading. Nothing you can say or do can make God work in you or for you in any way, because God is only present in you and *as* you. God can never be present any more in any time than this time. God is no more present in Jesus or any great teacher than in you, but you need to be present in God. You need to be alive and conscious of it. This is what consciousness really is!

We must work to dispel the magical illusion. Most of us have been so conditioned to this belief that it's very hard to change. We need to release the illusion of God sitting out there somewhere as a supreme person of the universe, waiting for you to prove your worthiness by faith. It doesn't make any difference to God whether you believe or not, but it makes a lot of difference to you, especially in terms of what you believe in and how you believe and what the direction of your faith may be. In other words, God is the omnipresent force of life and intelligence, and this force of life or intelligence must act. Not that it may act according to your belief in God, but that it must act. It can't help itself when you create the conditions that make the results inevitable.

When you throw the electrical switch and make the contact, electricity *must* flow. Not that it *may* flow if you're nice, if you're loving—it must flow, because we're dealing with law and not caprice. I think we weaken the process when we talk about the magic of believing. I know a lot of us have been conditioned to believe in the "magic of believing" and "miracle works of faith." These are lovely phrases, but I think they're clichés that religious people love to use. I think they weaken the whole process because we're dealing with law. There's no magic about it, there's no miracles involved, unless you are saying the rising and setting of the sun is a miracle, or that gravity is a miracle.

Some of you perhaps have a dimmer switch in your dining room where you turn the light up gradually and you have more light in the room, and you can also turn it down. You control the flow of the electrical current in the circuitry. When you turn the dimmer switch up and you get more light or power, this is no miracle. The power was law all the time. In the sense of faith dealing with the processes of life, positive faith simply tunes in to and turns on a power that is ever-present.

## FAITH IS NOT RELATIVITY BUT TRUTH

We've also been misled with the idea of the relativity of faith. We might say, "Oh, if I could just have more faith," or "If I could have faith like she has." "If I had that kind of faith I'd be able to do anything." Actually, our need is not for some gift of faith from somewhere, or for more of it, but the need is for the discipline to center your faith in Truth, to center your faith in that which is positive. To center your faith in the Allness of the infinite process.

I often say that the need in our life is to own our own consciousness. Essentially, to accept responsibility for our own lives. And if you say you lack faith, this is kind of a way of copping out through self-pity. It's like saying you can't make the basketball team because you're not tall enough. By making excuses, you're talking about the fact that this is just the way I am. This is the way I was born. I was a short person and therefore I can't get on a team that requires tall people. The fact is you are always tall in spirit, regardless of your physical stature. You always have faith, but how are you using it? How is your discipline?

Emmet Fox says don't think about the problem—think about God. This is what he called his Golden Key. Stop thinking of your insufficiencies and think of the all-sufficiency in God. Stop thinking of your illness and think of the Allness of healing life that is always present even within the illness. Center your attention, focus your consciousness upon the positive, and thus, there's a tremendous, faith-thinking power that flows through and enables you to do creative things.

## FAITH DOES NOT CHANGE REALITY BUT OUR PERCEPTION

Every once in a while, I get letters from radio listeners who ask, "Do you really believe you can transform your life through positive faith?" There's a changing process of light streaming in when you open a window. The light comes in, but we don't think of the change in terms of some miracle that's taken place. Faith does not change the nature of reality. Faith doesn't really change you, it only changes what you think you are; it changes what you appear to be. It doesn't change the reality of you, but it tunes in to that reality and lets it be released, and that's important. Otherwise, you start thinking about all sorts of other magical, miraculous things, like turning wine into water and water into wine, and blood into stones and stones into bread, and turning certain kinds of people into other kinds of people. This isn't what is involved; it isn't magic.

When people believed in a flat world during the pre-Columbian times, it was still round, whether they believed it or not. They just didn't know it, so they accepted it on the level of their perceptions. Their belief in a flat world did not change the round world one little bit, nor later to believe in a round world did not require making changes in the flat world. It simply became to them what they saw it as being. So it is with life, constantly.

When you pray for health, positive faith will not make an incurable condition well. Your faith has already been involved in the condition. Unconsciously and unwittingly, you are believing in the negative condition, and therefore it is becoming real to you. Positive faith simply turns from a focus on the negative appearance to centering of attention on the Allness of God Life. Now that Allness of God Life is always present. That's why Jesus says, "Judge not according to appearances, but judge righteous judgment" (John 7:24). We're not trying to change things, we're trying to refocus our attention from one thing to another, from the negative to the positive. But we're not trying to work magic. We're not trying to get blood out of a turnip. We're actually trying to allow the reality to be expressed and to be experienced at that level of the real. You are more than you appear to be, always. Positive faith is simply relating to the *more*. That's all. It's relating to the *more* of who you truly are.

When you say that faith enables you to release a tremendous new potentiality or human resource, it doesn't manufacture it from somewhere. It simply allows you to identify with yourself at a higher level, but that higher level was always present. It didn't suddenly become present because of your faith. When you understand that, then you know that wherever you are, whatever you're experiencing, there's always *more* in you. You may be in the midst of a situation in your job where you feel that you're inadequate, where you're not able to do the kind of thing you're supposed to do. Right at that moment there is more in you, and if that job is yours to do and if you've been drawn to it out of consciousness, then there is within you the power and potential to do the job and do it well—even if you've never been able to do it before.

Because there's always more in you, and if you can begin to relate to yourself and identify with yourself from the level of *more*, this is what faith does. You see your sickness, your limitation, your bad experiences, in a sense, like the flat world. It's your belief, based on your experience at that time. But there is a wholeness in you even as there's a round world within the flat world. One simply transcends the other. You have believed in darkness. By recentering in positive faith, you tend to reveal that which is real. You open the window to the light.

## FAITH OPENS A CHANNEL TO OUR TREMENDOUS POTENTIAL

Now, you also want to understand that there's always a tremendous transcendent level of spiritual awareness. This is at the depth of us and there's always a tremendous potential to do things beyond the seeming human ability. For instance, Henry David Thoreau talks about the fact that we can come ultimately to "live with the license of the higher order of beings." At the highest level of spiritual consciousness, we tune in upon a kind of vibration that enables us to sense things. In parapsychology, the talk is about ESP, extrasensory perception. But the fact is that everyone has these extra senses, even though we may not be aware of them; yet sometimes intuitively we sense them. But we all have the ability to suddenly see something that we haven't seen before, to suddenly become aware of something that is on the transcendent vibration, and faith simply frees up the communication process. It opens the way to allow us to function at the highest possible level, to function as a full spiritual being.

It is probably true that at the highest level of every individual there is this kind of communication potential. It is probably possible, but I don't say we should necessarily get involved in experimenting with this, because I think it will unfold naturally at the time it is right for us. Yet I believe if we were to get ourselves completely tuned in to a believing consciousness, centered in the dynamics of our own God Self, and begin to function at the highest possible level of perception, that we could then sit and communicate clearly and completely with someone around the world without a telephone.

Even so, I don't think we should dabble in that and try to develop that sort of thing unless it comes on us naturally. Otherwise, we become like the person who came to me a number of years ago who was a clairvoyant. She was not a professional clairvoyant, but she had what she called the "curse of clairvoyance." Long ago in life, she had discovered that she was able to read people's minds and foretell all sorts of fantastic things. But it was a millstone around her neck because she felt she could never be a normal, natural person. She could never communicate normally because she always knew what people were saying before they said it. It was so disturbing that the woman almost lost her mind as a result of it. I worked with her to try to bring it all into balance.

I say when these things are ready in consciousness, you'll begin to develop a higher awareness that will enable you to communicate on different levels. But the important thing is to know that there is always the potential. For instance, if you're sitting at home stewing and fretting over the fact that you've lost something and you can't figure out where it is, how important is it to know that you are one at the highest level of your being with Infinite Mind? When you center yourself in God Consciousness and allow the faith process to flow forth through you, it will open up your awareness so that suddenly you'll know. Suddenly, into your mind will come a vision of your keys sitting just exactly where you dropped them in the driveway. Or of some person who is just there waiting for you to call, and the contact is exactly what you needed. That potential is always present, and I think this is the marvelous thing that happens when we open up the communication process through quickening this awareness of faith. Not in some faith in magic, faith in impossibilities, but faith in moving at the highest level of vibration so we can begin to experience wonderful things in a normal, natural, easily discernible way, for example, living with the license of a higher order of beings.

## FEW OF US FULLY USE OUR GOD POWER

Few of us ever use more than a small part of the God Power within us. Usually this is because of a faulty self-evaluation, when we misjudge ourselves, put ourselves down, or typecast ourselves like an actor who's been involved in a particular role throughout a long period of time. We accept all sorts of standards based on past history and experience. "I know I can't do that because I never could." Well, that's like saying that to Thomas Edison after he failed 10 times. Edison would go on for 300 times, every time knowing that the failure simply evidenced the fact that he was closer to the potential of doing it perfectly.

It is no matter that you have failed at certain things, you may not be in your right place. It may not be the kind of experience you should be involved in, but don't look at yourself and say, "This is just an evidence of my limitations." Don't think of limitations, think of *limitlessness*. We've accepted what psychologists refer to as statistical laws of averages, where we were maybe told that the chances of success in business for the average person is about 1-in-7. If you start a business for yourself, your odds are pretty low if you're ever going to make a success of it, according to statistics.

In the same sense, we're often given the gloomy prediction of doom, such as that one out of every five is going to contract a dreaded disease in their lifetime, and these are computed irrefutably by the law of averages, so there's no hope for you. I say these things are fine in terms of looking backward and computing how things have worked. But why be an average person? Why accept that average? Why not say, "I'm going to live with the license of the higher order of beings." "I'm going to raise my consciousness above that level so that I'm not involved in that statistical outline." All the great achievements of civilization have been made by people who refused to consult statistics, who refused to listen to those who could prove that what they wanted to do, and what in fact they ultimately did do, was absolutely and completely impossible. But they would not accept the impossible. That's what happens in us when we engage the believing consciousness.

# According to Your Faith Be It Done Unto You

Jesus said, "According to your faith, be it done unto you" (Matthew 9:29). He's referring to the focus of attention. Sickness is according to your faith. Now that's hard for us to see because we've always thought of faith as something that relates to God. Faith is always present, and the focus of attention is in one direction or another, so sickness is according to your faith. Health and success are also according to your faith. The reason so many people continue in physical limitation or plod along in mediocrity is that they see so many obstacles and difficulties looming before them that they become discouraged and they give up. A person will often say, "Well, after all I'm only human, what can you expect?" You're not only human, and it's so important that we emphasize that. The human part of you is like a shell that encloses the divine of you. Creative faith relates to and releases the imprisoned splendor of your transcendent Self, much in the same way as the butterfly breaking out of the chrysalis. The Divine in you is always present. The Divine in you, which is the transcendent and the tremendous power by which you can do the kinds of things you dream of doing. The impossible dreams are always possible, if you listen deeply within yourself.

Don't emphasize your problems, the facts of past performance, or what we could call the evidence of impossibility. You certainly may have a need, and it's not positive to refuse to face the need, but a need has no built-in limitations. It doesn't come all wrapped up, neatly packaged with the evidence that you can't do this thing. No need ever comes into your life with built-in limitations. There are only limiting attitudes about it.

What do you think? What's your belief? What are you going to believe in? Impossibilities or possibilities? You can believe that life is a constant deterioration process for you, or you can believe that you're in the flow of an infinite, eternal life that is unfolding, progressing, freeing you from all limitations. What do you believe? Where is your faith?

If the Alps had looked as formidable to Napoleon as they did to his advisers, he would never have crossed them in midwinter. But he showed the focus of his attention when he said, "There shall be no Alps. I refuse to see them as limitations." He saw them only as opportunities to use his military genius, which he did.

## There Is a Tremendous Resource Right Where You Are

Right where you are, there is a resource of wisdom and substance. Right where you are, there is a resource of supply, of creativity, of ability, of tremendous ways through which you can do great things, always present right where you are. It enables you to do the kinds of things you need to do. Put your faith to work—your positive faith—in creative ways and start believing in yourself and the all-accomplishing power of God within you. Believe it and believe from it, act from that belief, and you will be amazed at the kinds of things that will take place in your life, the ways in which simple little every-day experiences will suddenly become easy and transcendent, and you'll begin to do things that you never believed you could do.

# You Can Only Be You

But let's be realistic about this power of believing. When Jesus says, "All things are possible to them that believe" (Mark 9:23), he was not saying that a swan could become a duck. He was not saying a nonmusical person could become a concert pianist. This is a very important thing, because often we get this carried out of context. He did not mean that you could do something that is not a part of your innate potentiality. You can only be you, and only you can be *you*, although through positive faith, you can release more of you than you've ever done. That's what we're talking about—not being somebody else, not taking on the potentialities that other people express—but knowing your own potentialities and releasing them and fulfilling them, releasing your own imprisoned splendor.

Many students of Truth are misled at this particular point, and it's so important that we get the concept straight. Quite often it is said, "You can do anything you want to do through faith. You can have anything you want to have through faith," and that's misleading because it's not true. You can only be you, and you can only do that which is the fulfilling potential of your life. If a person is too influenced by covetousness and allows herself to be stimulated by her covetousness, by her desire, her acquisitive instinct, by her materialistic and selfish interests, this will not release that splendor.

It is very important to grasp that if you are to acquire or to experience something that is not a part of your own innate flow, through the metaphysical law, then you lose even if you win. It's like in transplant surgery where they have what they call a rejection syndrome—the tissue will not take hold simply because there's a variance in the quality or the consciousness or the types of tissue that are present—they just won't take hold and there's a tendency to reject. You will somehow tend to reject or to find yourself unable to hold on to all that which you've acquired easily through this kind of false demonstration, where you've acquired something not a part of your own flow. Somehow through will-power and through the constant determination and through a lot of grasping, you can get all sorts of things in life, but there's no way you can ever really take hold of or become a part of that which is not really a part of you.

Faith is not a magical means of working miracles. Get that out of your consciousness. You are the great miracle, and the dynamics of faith is the key to the kingdom of your own potentiality. As Jesus said, "Seek first the kingdom and its righteousness and all the things shall be added" (Matthew 6:33). Not all things, but all the things that come easily out of your own divine flow, out of your own divine potential. Things that come to you easily because they are part of your own pattern, a part of your own unfoldment. The need is to listen to your own transcendence, to know yourself. This will lead you to desire to unfold that which you innately are and thus to fulfill your uniqueness.

Otherwise, when we say all things are possible, we don't mean, for instance, that carbon can become a good conductor of electricity, because carbon is not a good conductor. It's a very poor conductor of electricity. But a carbon filament can be used by electricity and fulfill its uniqueness. Just imagine a carbon filament saying, "I just can't conduct electricity like copper wire, so I'm no good. You can't expect me to make a light." But you see, Jesus did not say, "*Make* your light shine." He said, "*Let* your light shine."

For the carbon filament, we might say, the question is: Are you willing to be used as an instrument? And if it agrees and acquiesces in the whole thought, then behold, "Let there be light!"

I think this illustration is important to really understand faith. Faith doesn't make the light by some magic process, faith doesn't even make the filament a good conductor for that which will become light. Faith simply makes the contact and turns on the switch. The power is there, the process is there, the whole conduit is there. The whole activity of the intended process is always present. It simply makes the contact.

God is centered in you. God is centered in you always. What is your consciousness centered in? If your thought is centered in materiality, if it's centered in difficulties, if it's centered in the news of the day, it's centered in the idea *Oh, my! Everything happens to me*, and this is going to frustrate the whole flow. God is centered in you. The kingdom of all potentiality is already within you. Positive faith is the key to the kingdom. You don't need to become something different to release your imprisoned splendor.

Your need is simply to get your consciousness centered in God, centered in the realization that the whole universe believes in you. The whole universe is flowing into and through you. Your need is to accept it, to let it happen, and to let yourself be directed out of that consciousness in a faith-believing attitude. To know you are a spiritual being and so armed with this believing attitude, you can proceed to go about your business, doing the things that need to be accomplished, and doing them easily. You do them out of the flow of your own consciousness of the divine process that's working in you.

# Realize That God Is Centered in You

Start the day, every day of your life, in a very disciplined way. Start the day by taking time to be still. And in the stillness, get to the realization that God is centered in you. Quietly realize, "God is centered in me." If you want to put it another way, "God believes in me." "The whole universe believes in me, and I can know that because I'm breathing, I'm living, and I'm alive. I'm the activity of God expressing as me, so God is centered in me." Just be aware of that.

## 'God Believes in Me'

*"I believe from this consciousness of centering process in God. I am centered in God, and out of the centering, I know I have the capacity to do all the things that need to be done. I know I can release a guidance activity that will enable me to make the steps that I should take, make the contacts that I need to, do the kinds of things that are before me this day and do them easily and do them well, because I'm in tune with a process that's always present, never absent. I believe and I act from that believing attitude. And as I go out in the everyday in this consciousness, I will find that I will be confident, I will be less. There can be no fear. There can be no anxiety. There can be no worry. There can be no hesitation along the way of life, because I know the activity of God is flowing easily through me."*

Get that feeling in at the beginning of your day, that the whole universe believes in you. The whole universe believes in you as a worker who is successful and efficient and effective. You go off to your work that day knowing that this divine process is flowing through the cells and functions of your body and tingling through your fingertips. When you go to your job, this activity is flowing through you because you know you're in tune and you know that attunement keeps you constantly in the flow of the divine process. This is essentially what faith is. It's not talking about it, not saying "I believe." It's doing it. It's expressing it. It's releasing it, easily. You turn the switch and the dynamic process of the activity of God flows easily through you and all your ways wherever you go.

Commit yourself to this: Decide right now that you're going to practice this faith this week. Not that you're going to talk to people about faith and tell everybody about what great faith you have. As American poet Eddie Guest used to say, "I'd rather see a sermon than hear one any day." So rather than tell people about faith, or talk about how much you're going to try to have it, just do it. Do it by realizing that God is centered in you and the whole universe has faith in you and allow that faith process to direct you with your attitudes, with your feelings, your moods, your motivations. You will find that this will be a very successful week. Not only that, but you will be open to a whole new dimension in your life.

## MEDITATION—GOD IS CENTERED IN YOU

*Let's be still and get this feeling that God is centered within you. There's nothing you can do about it. You can't create it, you can't change it, you can't alter it, you can't make it any more real. This is true spiritual reality. As Plotinus put it, the whole universe is rushing, streaming, pouring into you from all sides while you just sit quiet.*

*The universe is centered in you. All love, all power, all life, all creativity is centered in you right now. This is the reality of you, and as you think about it and believe it, then you're centered in this process. You're centered in God and you make a contact. And thus through your life, through your mind, through your heart, through your hands, there's a flow of dynamic activity. It is the natural activity of your life. You're simply releasing that which is really yours, and you allow it to flow. So we see you right now going forth from this place today, in tune with this God activity. It is the dynamic potential of your own being, effectively released, so that you can do the kinds of things you need to do and do them easily, do them effectively, and do them successfully and fulfillingly.*

*You will do this, and we're grateful for this consciousness. Let's just for a moment feel grateful that God is centered in you, that the universe believes in you, grateful that you are a glorious, wonderful instrument through which the creative process flows easily and fulfillingly.*

# 6

---

# LOVE

## THE DESIRE TO BE MORE

"IN EVERY PERSON there lives an image of what he ought to be. As long as he is not that image, he ne'er at rest will be." This is the poetic thought of Friedrich Ruckert. It's very likely that you are reading this book because you have a desire to grow. You may not be consciously aware that this was your motivation in picking it up, but secretly, within yourself, there's a tremendous desire to be more. There's a feeling of inability to rest content with what you are.

This is what I call "divine discontent," and it's a restlessness which is a part of the lives of all of us. Intuitively, you know that there is more in you. Probably all that we can do is to serve as a midwife to help you give birth to that *more*.

# THE COSMIC PROCESS OF LOVE

In our study of the laws of metaphysics, we may be excited about the new insight in Truth, we may be extremely interested, intrigued with the positive ideas of consciousness, of positive thinking, of the power of the spoken word, of faith, and these wonderful insights. However, not until we comprehend and begin to work with the cosmic process of love does Truth become a way of life and living for us. I'm sure that many of you have read or at least can quickly recall Paul's 13th chapter in First Corinthians. If you have not read it, then we'll let that be a part of the homework assignment for this chapter.

A dynamic treatise on love and among other things, Paul sums up some spiritual achievements and then he says, "If with these things you have not love, you are nothing," and that's pretty emphatic. He doesn't say that without love you're going to have difficulties in life. He says, "Without love you are nothing." It's pretty blunt, but it helps us to understand that the whole concept of love is much more than emotions, much more than senses and feelings and sexual involvements. It's so much deeper than all of this.

Love is the completeness of life. Jesuit priest Pierre Teilhard de Chardin refers to it as "the totalization of life." On many occasions Jesus makes a statement, "Love one another," but this is not expressed because it is a nice Sunday school moral to love people. What he's really saying is that you should love because when you are not giving expression to love, you are out of the flow of the cosmic process of love, out of the flow of the divine rhythm.

You're not in tune with the very specific power that enables you to live vitally and abundantly. When you give way to love, when you allow this cosmic flow to come forth within you, then you are synchronized with this tremendous transcendent process, and you enter the dimension of divine completion, the totalization that only love can experience in you.

What is love? Whatever we think it is, love is the actual expression of being loving. It's nonverbal. It's something that is beyond definition.

## THE QUEST FOR LOVE

When you've been conditioned to believe that we come into life empty and we go forth into the world to be filled, we're empty creatures. We have nothing. We're born helpless and hopeless, and yet our lives are molded and shaped by what our parents do to us, what the schools do to us, what life does to us, and how society influences us. We go to school to get knowledge. We go to church to get religion. We go out into the marketplace to get money and to make our fame and fortune, and we look to special people for love.

So in this commonplace viewpoint, love is a needed commodity, and it's so important to us. It's vital that we find someone to give us love, and if we find that one, then we have love to give, but if we don't find people who give us love, then we're empty and devoid of love and that's what's wrong with our lives. Loves comes naturally to us when we find the right person to love or to be loved by. This is the way our reasoning goes about this consciousness of love, *and it's all erroneous.* This isn't what love is at all.

Life for most people is a long quest for love. We're always looking for love here and there and everywhere—in experiences, in relationships. "Oh, someday I'm going to find my love. Across the crowded room, love comes into my life." Life becomes a quest for objects of love, and in human consciousness, I'm sure we all realize that this is where we are much of the time.

# LOVE IS AN INNER POWER, NOT AN OBJECT

Intuitively, within ourselves we know that love is an inner power, not an object; that our need is not to *be* loved. Our need is *to* love. Within every person there's a hunger and a thirst to express love, to radiate love, to get ourselves in tune with the cosmic flow at the root of our being, to simply plug in, to turn the lights on, and to express out of the overflow of this inner love a lovingness toward life. We have a hunger for this, but we don't understand the process, so instead we're out looking for it somewhere else, while all the time it's within us.

We've been misled to a large extent by psychological teachings that claim the greatest need of man is to be loved, that somehow suggest love is a commodity rather than a cosmic process. We simplistically suppose that our lives lack love because we have not been loved enough, so it's easy to put the blame on our parents, on our teachers, on our environment. The fact that our father mistreated us and our mother did not love us becomes the reason for all of the scars and all of the problems in our life. It's so easy to get into this kind of shallow, psychoanalytical conclusion, which is simplistic. Furthermore, we need to unlearn the error of thinking of love in this sense.

## GOD IS LOVE AND I AM THAT LOVE

We need to redefine this thing called love, or rather *undefine* it, to get it out of the terms of definitions. We've accepted the biblical statement "God is love" as if love were a commodity that God has. So God gives it to us, and then we have it, and we pass it along to other people. Actually, it is more a description of what God is than what God does. God is love is expressed much in the same way as God is life, God is intelligence, God is power, God is love.

You see, these are simply abstract generalizations until we know whatever else God is, God is me. Does that surprise you a little bit? Whatever else God is, God is me. I am the activity of God expressing itself as me. God is life, and I am life manifesting as my body temple. God is intelligence, and I am that intelligence in the form of the wisdom of my mind. God is power, and I am that power in the form of my strength and my creativity, my ability to form and shape and build. God is love, and I am that love expressing in and through and as my loving heart.

## MY LOVE IS MY ATTUNEMENT WITH THE COSMIC FLOW

But I have no love of my own. My love is my attunement with the cosmic flow, which is centered in the great heart of the universe. It is not love that is the greatest need in our lives, but loving, giving way to this cosmic flow of love. It's not the need of being loved by people so that people can give us this commodity. Love is to touch the deep spring of our own nature, turn our own lights on, and be love.

Be what we really are, which was Meister Eckhart's thought when he said, "Let God be God in you. Let love be love at the root of your being."

## I Am Created in and of Love

We need to continuously remind ourselves of our roots, of our divine origins. We think all too much about being a child of these parents or a child of misfortune or a child of certain difficult experiences. We need to realize that we are a child of God. To know that we're rooted in this divine process so that when we get the realization we were created in God's image and likeness, this is the divine imprint. Yet this is little more than a cliché unless we personalize it.

It's not nearly enough to say, "I'm created in God's image and likeness." We need to hunger and thirst for God, to know God created me in his image and God is love and therefore I am created in and of love. It's my nature. It's the root of my being. God loves me. God is love in me, and I am the very activity of love and expression, which means I have within me all the love in the universe. No loving person ever lived who had more love than I do! That's hard to accept because we've conditioned ourselves to feel that we've been bereft of love, that we haven't been loved enough.

I have within me all the love in the universe. I have enough love, enough centering energy within me to love every person and situation, simply because every person and every situation is also created in and of love. Love is the heart and root of all things. There's no such thing as an absence of love. There's only a frustration of it. There's only a case of, as Jesus puts it metaphorically, "Hiding our lamp under a bushel" (Matthew 5:15).

## THERE IS NO STRAIN OR DRAIN IN THE LOVING

It's important to know that to love someone, when we say, "I love this person," I'm not giving them something. I'm not taking something that I have and giving it to them so that now I have less because they have more. There's no strain or drain in the loving. Now you've heard it, and you may have expressed it yourself unthinkingly and perhaps self-pityingly: "I have loved and loved and loved until I am just exhausted."

But if a person feels a sense of strain or drain in the loving, it's because he is out of tune with his own inner flow. He's trying in human consciousness, through willpower, to overcome things his consciousness is basically centered on, but he's out of the love flow. Loving another person is simply feeling yourself in the divine flow within you, seeing out of that consciousness to the divine flow, sending yourself in the divine flow with him and seeing the Divine within him. It is love within me uniting with love within him. If we love each other, then I love out of the depths of my love, he loves out of the depths of his love, and there's a union and a communion.

There's no exchange of anything, there's only an intermingling of sight, intermingling of consciousness, and it's so important that we understand this. If I have a feeling of love for another person, it is because I have, to that degree, felt a sense of love within myself, therefore I love that person out of my own self-love, and I must feel good about myself. If I don't feel good about myself, I can't really feel good about another, and vice versa.

## Love From the Divine Flow of a Cosmic Consciousness

Love has become a great cliché. It's a plaything of human volition. We talk about it, we sing about it, and it's all up in human consciousness, all in the emotions, all in the senses, but cut off from the Divine Source, from the divine flow.

This is why we have such problems in our human relationships. As a commodity, I cannot give love to anyone, and no one can give love to me. Now don't misunderstand this. I can be loving. I can create a loving environment. I can bathe this person in the light of love as I see this person in love, but I do not exchange anything. I don't feel any loss because I've loved this person. Nothing has gone out of me, but when I love a person in that consciousness, then that person likely feels relaxed, feels secure, feels able to let down his own natural resistance, which is always the only problem we have in our lives.

As people let down their resistance, they commune with the light of love within themselves, and love flows easily for and through them. They love themselves, and I love myself, only in a transcendent way, in a spiritual sense. Out of this consciousness of self-love and seeing in the light of love, then there's a comingling, and a beautiful relationship ensues, but it's a relationship that is built on a foundation, on a root consciousness, of the divine flow of this cosmic process.

## LOVE IS THE WAY WE SEE OUR NEIGHBOR

How important it is to realize at the central core of Truth, that the teaching of Truth is love. This is the central core of Jesus' teaching. This is what he talks about most of the time, but we miss the point if we think of love as something that is a thing, something that is given, exchanged, or something that is a commodity.

Remember, Jesus says, "Love thy neighbor," and of course, this is a great cliché. It's a fundamental part of religious tradition and it's something that you must always love your neighbor no matter who your neighbor is. We have all the clichés of people who say, "I love my neighbor, as long as I can choose who the neighbor's going to be and who I live next door to." The point is, this idea of loving one's neighbor tends to give us problems because we say, "How can I love people who I don't like?" It's like being asked to go out on the street and give money to strangers.

This is the way we've thought of love. I don't mind giving money to a friend, but I don't want to take something out of my pocket and give it to someone I don't even know and don't care for, someone who I'm sure is going to misuse it. Actually, the phrase, "Love thy neighbor," in the Hebrew Bible should be translated, "Love to your neighbor." It's an entirely different thing as it means not giving something to him but *acting lovingly toward him.* This is the intent of the commandment, not love him but be loving. To love him deals with something you give him or something you do to him, but being loving deals more with what goes on in your attitude, your perception. It's the way you see him, not something you bestow upon him.

Jesus makes it more emphatic when he goes on to say, "Love your neighbor as yourself." The manner in which you treat the neighbor comes out of the esteem in which you hold yourself. You cannot know and love another person truly, unless you know and love yourself. That's why he says, "Love your neighbor as yourself." Be loving to your neighbor out of the overflow of your own innate awareness of self-love.

## THE EMPHASIS OF LOVE IS ON YOU

Loving is keeping in the flow of the cosmic process. It's letting your light shine, keeping the lights turned on, not because the world needs the light—and it probably does—not because your family needs the light—and they probably do—but because you need to keep your light turned on. Otherwise, you and your own consciousness are going to suffer. This is the key. If you're not sending it in love, then you're not letting yourself be loved, and you are dependent on whether some other person acts lovingly toward you.

In that common consciousness, every change in people and every changing condition in your relationship is a threat that triggers in you a reaction of hate or resistance. You're always thinking about, "What are they going to do?" or you feel jealous or upset or angry because I've loved this person but he hasn't responded. He hasn't returned it.

If you feel a sense of ingratitude over the fact that someone doesn't seem to return or reciprocate your love, then you really didn't love. You were bartering. You were looking for attention. You were looking for something from him. And that's a hard lesson, but that's the kind of lesson that is implicit in this consciousness of Truth.

## LOVE YOUR ENEMIES BECAUSE YOU DESERVE IT

Jesus carries the process further yet. He says, "You have heard it said of old, love your neighbor and hate your enemy, but I say unto you, love your enemies and pray for those that despitefully use you that you may be sons of your Father" (Matthew 5:43-44).

Now this is too much for many of us. It's nice to get a consciousness where you can be loving and can express love to lovable people, but to love enemies, to love people who despitefully use you, that's the very consciousness and concept that has caused a lot of folks to turn away from Truth and the teachings of Jesus.

"Love your enemies and pray for those that persecute ... That you may be sons of your Father." The key is here but it's rarely seen: Love your enemy not because he's deserving of it. The point is, love your enemy not because he deserves it, but because *you* deserve it.

Again, the emphasis is on you. If you are upset and confused and bitter and resentful and resistant and fearful and angry because of an enemy, the basic problem in terms of the cosmic idea is that you have enmity, and the enmity is in you, not in him. Now he may have done all sorts of things, and you may want to get the law against him, and you maybe should do that, but the important thing is: What is going on in you? If you have enmity, you have a problem. You have a red light as long as you hold that enmity and you're going to suffer the consequences.

Jesus says, "Resist not that which is evil." He also says, "Go the second mile," not because this is a nice thing to do in the world, but because you have to be very sure that you do not allow yourself to be centered in a conflict. Turn off the flow because the process that makes for life and vitality and harmony and health and all the good things that we desire depends upon keeping the contact within yourself in the centered flow of love, the "totalization process."

Jesus again is centered with you. If you resist or resent, you frustrate the flow within yourself. We withhold love regardless of the reason for it, and we can think of lots of reasons why we should not love certain persons, but to withhold love regardless of the reason is to withhold the vital power, the only power, by which you can be healthy and happy and successful.

Just like the old saying, "You can't have your cake and eat it too." You can't have your enmity and have health. You can't have your conflict with people, your resistance and your resentment, and still have peace or have the kind of flow that makes for success and harmony in your relationships and your affairs. There's no way. You can't have both.

## GET OUT OF A CONSCIOUSNESS OF RESISTANCE

We may think at times that we have good reason not to love someone because of what they have done. However, we can never afford to entertain thoughts that separate us from the flow of divine love. Jesus uses a metaphor that is often misunderstood. It's one of these things that either is taken out of context or else it's totally overlooked.

He says, "If thy right eye causes thee to stumble, pluck it out. If thy right hand cause thee to stumble, cut it off" (Matthew 5:29-30). I suspect there were fundamentalist fanatics who literally believed that this is what you should do, cut off your hand if you found yourself getting involved with some sort of resentment, but this isn't what Jesus was talking about.

He's simply saying, "Stop thinking negative thoughts." If you resist someone, don't be so concerned with why he is causing you resistance, but why are you resisting? Get out of the consciousness of resistance. If you're upset, then it's because you're easily upset. Why are you upset? What's wrong within you? If he has done something, you say, "He's done this to me. Why does he do that to me? Why does he say those things to me?"

I always say that "to me" is the little fishhook. That's the barb that hangs you up. In other words, in the first place, get rid of the fishhook, pluck it out, cut it off, and then ask the question again, "Why did he do it?" Not to me, he didn't do it to me. He did it. If it's to me, it's because I got hung up in my reaction, in my resistance. Why did he do it? If I can see him objectively and ultimately, I can see him lovingly and I can see he did it because he's confused. He did it because of certain problems in his own life, a feeling of lack of love in his own consciousness. He's cut off from this inner flow of love himself, and he's lashing out at life.

If I can understand that, I keep myself free. I cut it off, pluck out the eye, get rid of the limitation in my own consciousness, and then I can say to myself, "First of all, in my love flow and out of that love flow, I can see him lovingly." It doesn't mean I condone what he does, it doesn't mean that I have to let him go free if he'd broken the law. It means that I cannot help the world or anybody, and certainly myself, if I try at all costs to cause someone to pay the last farthing at the expense of my own self. Then you have two frustrated people. You have two people out of the flow. The important thing is I must keep myself centered, keep myself in tune, and then out of that centering consciousness, I can be an influence. Then I can help, then I can radiate the consciousness of peace to people in the world.

## WHEN TO SALUTE THE DIVINITY IN OTHERS

It is wonderful to salute the divinity in another person. Today we use this Hindustani term *namaskar* to acknowledge this divinity. It simply means "the divinity within me salutes the divinity within you."

It's great to know that you're saluting the divinity in people, but the time to salute the divinity in people is the very time when it's most difficult to do. If someone has irritated you, that's the time to get the namaskar consciousness, not because he deserves it but because if you're irritated, it is an evidence that you're out of tune, and you can't afford to be out of tune.

Even many of our medical doctors will tell us this today. Psychologists will tell you that. Anybody who's involved in the psychosomatic processes of illness will tell you that any time you get out of tune, you're going to experience headaches and stomach ulcers and all sorts of problems. You can't afford it. The point is, the time to say *"Namaskar,* I salute the divinity within you" sincerely is the very time when you're upset, when you're angry, when you're inclined to say anything but *namaskar.*

## FUNCTIONING AT THE LEVEL OF LIFE'S COMPLETION

The important thing is that when you keep centered in your own love flow, you begin to function at the level of life's completion. This is why Teilhard calls it the "totalization process." You cannot function as a total being unless you're in tune with love. It's so important because suddenly when you're in tune with love, you experience what Henry David Thoreau calls the "license of a higher order of beings." Suddenly, then, you can experience life at its fullest. Suddenly you can experience life at the depth and the height of your own potential. You can do all sorts of things that otherwise you couldn't do, and you'll be protected from all sorts of things that otherwise you might unthinkingly experience.

## EXAMPLE OF SEEING A FRIEND IN CONSCIOUSNESS OF LOVE

Some time ago, a man told me of his own problem that showed the demonstrating power of love's transcendence in a way that was quite unique. It seems that a writer friend wanted to write the story of a very unusual incident that this man had been involved in, so he asked the man for his permission.

The man felt sure that certain phrasings of the story might be embarrassing and even harmful to other people involved, so he refused to let the writer publish the story, but the writer was furious because he'd already written the story. He'd put a lot into it, and he thought it was something very important and very good, so he said some very unpleasant things, and he stomped off in anger.

This was disturbing to this particular man because this friendship meant a lot to him. They'd been friends for many years, and they really liked one another. He struggled with his conscience because he wanted to do the right thing.

He weighed in the balance the process, and he felt tempted for a while to say, "Oh, well, I want my friendship more than anything," but he stood by his principle.

After some time, he finally realized that he was going to have to get himself straightened out. He began to take frequent times in stillness to deal with himself. He forgot about the friend for a while, and this is what he realized: It took time and stillness to get himself centered in the consciousness of love. It took time to get himself filled with the realization that in this divine flow of love, there can be no separation, there can be no confusion. There can be no ill will, no hurt, no anger. He waited until he could get himself completely at ease in this consciousness before he did anything further.

Then what did he do? He simply looked up from his consciousness and looked out and looked at his friend across the miles and saw him with eyes of love, saw him in the consciousness of love.

He didn't try to send anything to him. He didn't try to project any thoughts. He didn't try to speak a lot of words across the miles. He just sat with him in the consciousness of love, and within 48 hours, a letter came saying that the friend had suddenly felt very foolish in his attitude. The talk led to his talking to a lawyer about it, and the lawyer told him that he might have opened himself to charges of libel if he had published the article as he'd wanted to. He apologized.

He even thanked the man for committing himself to the process of Truth, to holding to that which was right and saving him from a great deal of unpleasantness and saying, incidentally, "I'm so glad that our friendship has not been destroyed, and I can hardly wait to see you again."

## HOW LOVE DOES ITS HEALING WORK

In a sense, love had done its healing, totalizing work, but let's take a look at what happened. Love didn't go out to where he lived in San Francisco, shake him up, and make him know that he was wrong. That's all in human consciousness.

Quite often we bring that thought into us when we come in the truth and we carry it over, blasting it over with metaphysics. The need is not to change people, not to set them right or to straighten them out, but to see them rightly and straighten out our own projected consciousness.

The only wrong involved as far as I'm concerned is that I'm seeing out of a negative consciousness. I have to straighten that out, and that's all I can ever do. When I straighten out my thoughts and get myself centered in the consciousness of love, not a love that is human, not a love that is willful, but a love that is attuned to the divine flowing, which is not mine at all but simply the overflow of a divine process within me, it's all I can ever do.

When I get centered in that consciousness, I feel good, I feel compassionate, and it's a case of "Love your enemies, love those who spitefully use you." Love wherever there are difficulties. I feel compassion, and the compassion is not so much what I'm giving the person as what I'm giving way to within myself. And suddenly out of that consciousness of compassion, I see clearly. I see clearly and out of that clear sight, I see through eyes of love.

I simply see from the consciousness of love, and suddenly I create the environment, and that's all you ever do in a loving relationship. It creates a loving environment. It doesn't make a difference whether it's the man next door or the man on the other side of the world or the man in the moon. It doesn't matter. There's no separation in truth. I create an environment in which suddenly he feels secure and he can let his own inner consciousness express, and suddenly there is an influence that is almost unbelievable.

He doesn't know what's happening. It's not that he's being brainwashed, not that he's being hypnotized. Nothing like that is happening at all, but suddenly there's a feeling of freedom in which he can see himself. He gives up his resistance. He gives up his willfulness, he sees clearly and he begins to see with eyes of love, and suddenly there's understanding.

Whenever two people really see each other, clearly and truly, out of a consciousness of love, there's always understanding. This is what understanding really is.


## RESISTANCE AND CHAOS

You see that when you resist a thing, when you fight a thing, you function at the lowest level of consciousness, and you send out and receive the most negative of vibrations, and we do this unconsciously. Even people who are trying to project thoughts of love often are projecting thoughts other than love, covering it up with platitudes of love.

Actually, they're really resisting and pretending. "Why doesn't he change? I love him." Quite often we say, "I'm going to love him even if it kills me." It's unfortunate that we'd make such a statement because by and large that's exactly what can happen, because it's that destructive. But our need is to stop resisting it, to cut off the hand, pluck out the eye, as Jesus says metaphorically—get out of the negative reaction.

Instead, enter the totalizing vibration of love, which is not your love, not human love, not willful love, but it's a cosmic process that flows through you. Your negative feelings fade away. The sense of urgency to change something fades away and you'll begin to see the clouds dissolve and the sun break through. Suddenly, there's understanding.

As you keep centered in the cosmic flow of love, you're not only protected but a "miracle" change takes place in all those whom you feel have had any kind of enmity toward you.

In today's world there's this consciousness of walking under a shadow everywhere that becomes almost an attracting force. One of the things we need to understand—and I know that most of us understand it intellectually, but we need to get this understanding deep within our consciousness—that as Job says, "That which I fear comes upon me." That which I resist, that which I'm even trying to change through love, is underneath a resistance and a resentment and is actually going to destroy me.

When you're out of the vibration of love, you're in a consciousness in which chaos is always a possibility. It doesn't mean that you've created the situation, but the situation can happen if you have that potential in yourself because you were out of the center of your own love vibration. If there is fear and anxiety then pluck it out, cut it off. These are danger signals that should never be ignored. Never allow yourself to go very long being fearful or anxious. You may cover up your fear and anxiety by all sorts of metaphysical platitudes, but that's not enough.

Pluck it out, get rid of it. Get yourself centered in the consciousness of love and know that in your love center, there's security, there's freedom from all harm, from all difficulties, from all confusion because you're centered in God, and God is love.

## Never Try to Love Anyone

Remember that love is not giving something. It is being something. Out of your insecurity and lack of self-love, you tend to resist the idea of loving the enemy. You may say, "I try to love this person, but it's hard."

I say to that person, "Don't *try* to love at all. Never *try* to love anyone." Quite often people who get involved in the cosmic process of love in an intellectual sense, say, "Well, I guess my need is to love everyone, so wherever I go, I'm trying to love this person."

I say, "Don't try to love anybody," because to try to love is not to love. If you're trying to love, it's in human consciousness. If you try to love, it's a judgment. You say, "He's terrible, but I'm going to try to love him." There's no way that you can love him through trying to love him if you've already established the realization that he's terrible.

To try to love is not to love. To try to love is human. Don't try to love, ever. Don't try, *let*. To try is something you're doing, something you're giving. Letting is something you are allowing, something that you're simply being a channel for. This is the kind of thing that many of you have come to experience in testing the biofeedback equipment, where you put these little electrosensors on and try to make a needle move up by changing the heat in your hand and so forth. When you try to do it, it doesn't work. Instead of the needle going up, it'll go down. But if you envision yourself doing it and then get into a consciousness of what I call "I don't give a dime," it's sort of a divine indifference, but you see yourself doing it. Just the exact opposite of trying, it's letting. Suddenly, it happens. The temperature changes, the needle goes up. It's beautiful, and that's exactly what happens in the flow of love. Don't try to love.

Stop trying to love. Get yourself centered, block the situation out, and stop looking at the person. Get yourself centered so you realize you're one with the divine flow, loved with an everlasting love by the infinite process that can never be anything else but love in you, because God is love and you're created in the love of God. You're created in love.

## THE ENVIRONMENT CREATED BY SEEING WITH LOVE

Let this consciousness become filled with your true nature, and then out of this consciousness, you simply open your eyes and see.

You see, but not with human judgment. Remember, Jesus said, "Judge not according to appearances but judge with righteous judgment" (John 7:24). You don't see it with human judgment. Suddenly you see almost with a spiritual peripheral vision that enables you to see beyond the limitation. Beyond the outward evidences that are causing you problems, you see what a person really is in Truth, and you see them in that consciousness.

You see them in a consciousness of love and you create, without trying to, an environment in which the person suddenly feels secure, and he can let down his guard. Most of the hostilities, most of the confusion that emanates from people comes because of fear. A person is resisting other people and things because he doesn't feel adequate. But if he's surrounded with a supportiveness of this sight of love, this insight of love, he feels secure.

Then he allows his resistances to fall. His defenses fall away and out of this comes the ability, the free expression of his divine potential—the Christ Potential. This may not happen overnight, but wonders do come through letting the cosmic process flow.

## THE EYE AS A FOUNTAIN

The interesting thing is, this all involves the ability to see. I've used this expression often and it's a very important thing. We'll sum it up with this right now. The word *eye* comes from a Hebrew root word, which is defined and translated as "fountain." Throughout the scriptures you often hear the statement, "The fountain of the eye. The eye is a fountain."

Seeing from a psychological point of view is taking images from the outside and having them plant themselves on the nerve endings of the inner eye itself, so that you're getting outward evidences in your consciousness. But transcendent seeing is a fountain that flows as the eye looks out into the world like a spotlight. A spotlight doesn't give anything out here, but it reveals things out there because of the light that it expresses.

The eye is a fountain, and when you see out of this inward attunement with the cosmic flow, whatever you look upon suddenly is illuminated, not because you're a holy person but because you're wholly in tune with the divine flow. You see differently and when you see differently, the fountain of that consciousness flows forth and the other person feels it. You may not know how it happened. It's not because you've said a lot of words of Truth or mouthed a lot of affirmations.

When you simply see someone in a consciousness of love, without any intellectual process at all, and out of that comes the clearing of your own resistance and resentment, suddenly an environment takes place and your friend feels relaxed and unthreatened and she expresses what she really can be.

## SEE WITH THE EYES OF LOVE

So, practice seeing with eyes of love. First, in an impersonal way. Do it impersonally as you're sitting in a subway or bus and you see someone opposite you. Pick the person who would be the most difficult to salute the divinity within, and let that be your little exercise.

Close your eyes. Don't try to love him. Close your eyes and get centered, and get the feeling of oneness with this divine flow until you feel that warmth of compassion flowing forth through you. Then open your eyes and think of this compassion, this consciousness flowing forth, not bringing the image out there in here, but flowing forth from here like a light. A light that is revealing things that otherwise you can't see. Don't try to see changes. Don't try to see things happen. Don't let the ego get involved.

Let it go. Just see with eyes of love, and then turn away and try it in another situation you're seeing. We often want to see it happen and get some credit for it. We want to be able to say, "Hey, you know what I did on the subway the other day? I looked at a guy and he changed overnight."

Don't look at it in that sense. Just get clear. Get yourself in tune and see with eyes of love. Practice this and then when you feel you're beginning to be adept at it, then practice it upon those close to you. Your errant son, your husband who's been a problem to you, or your boss or your coworkers, and look at them with eyes of love, and you'll begin to see that the first and foremost thing that will happen is that changes will take place in you. Your own consciousness, your own attitudes, and changes will begin to take place miraculously out here, and you'll wonder how it ever happened.

"I didn't do anything," and of course you didn't. "I of myself can do nothing, but the Father within does the works." This is basically what it's all about.

## MEDITATION—YOU ARE CENTERED IN LOVE

*Let's be still for just a moment and in this stillness, I want us to just remember that scriptural injunction, "Behold, I have loved thee with an everlasting love" (Jeremiah 31:3). You are loved. You are the activity of the divine process of love flowing forth through you, and as you, and right now you are centered in that contact with the inner flow of cosmic love—thus all the love in the universe is at your command. No one in all the world has any more love than you, and yet it's not something to give away.*

*It's something to enable you to feel secure, and an energy process so that you can see through this consciousness, see life in general, see the world out there. Even in the mundane things that the news accounts reveal, in the people around you, and the people close to you, you can see in all this the consciousness of love. In this consciousness, you're going to find freedom that you've never known before. Praise God for the Truth that makes us free.*

# 7

## PRAYER

### THE UNIVERSAL CALL TO PRAYER

THE CALL TO prayer is heard in many languages, and certainly through many religions. It may be an involvement with the throwing of sticks by a Confucianist. It may be the prayer wheel of Buddhism. It may be the voice from the tower calling the Muslim to pray as he prostrates himself toward the East. It may be the saying of a Mass. It may be a Native American standing on a hillside with his arms outstretched toward the moon as he prays in a consciousness of celebrating the whole universe. It may be a student of Truth expressing an affirmation.

The phrase "pray about it" is so perfunctorily used that it often becomes little more than a cliché. It implies engaging in a ritual or a public ceremony that is experienced through a position of the body, or by an intonation of the voice, or verbally by route. I love the comment of Sidney Harris, a syndicated news columnist. He whimsically says, "How God must laugh at the catatonic poses people put themselves into when a public prayer or invocation is recited, as if He were a general out there reviewing the troops."

Prayer often also implies a last-ditch effort, which is reminiscent of Shakespeare's *The Tempest* where the words are expressed, "All lost, all lost, to prayers, to prayers." There is no hope, so now we might as well ask God for help. It would remind us of the old group drama where, in a crisis, the dramatist might swing at God from the wings to disentangle a desperate situation.

## A METAPHYSICAL PERSPECTIVE ON PRAYER

As I have outlined in recent lessons, metaphysics is a way of thinking, and as I want to clearly point out, it is also a way of praying. However, I think we need to understand what is implied by the word *prayer*. We might consult a dictionary, but it really wouldn't be too much help. The dictionary says, or indicates, how the word has been submerged in stereotypes as it defines *prayer* as, "to entreat, to implore, to supplicate, as to God." Other words used are: *intercession*, *exhortation*, *invocation*, *benediction*, and on and on we could go. But obviously this tends to imply an attempt to deal with God out there somewhere, God who is separate, God who is apart. God who is the Big Person in the sky, like the giant creature of Michelangelo's artwork on the ceiling of the Sistine Chapel in Rome.

But you see, this is the problem. While we can understand the relationship, which will imply a metaphysical system, it's important to let go of this absence of God image—as Ralph Waldo Emerson beseeches, "so God may fire us with his presence." We need to get away from the thought of God *somewhere*, and think of God as *present*, active within us, expressing himself *as* us. We must let go of the tendency to pray *to* God, to reach *for* God, to supplicate help *from* God, and to get to the realization that God is present as the Allness in which I exist and you exist as an eachness. These are not just words, this is a realization that we must work to realize. It's important to let go of the "say your prayers" technique. Prayer is not conditioning God with your needs, begging for handouts from heaven. Rather, prayer is conditioning your life with the activity of God, causing a change in your tendency, your consciousness, and your awareness, so that you can acknowledge that which already is.

Jesus clearly says, "The Father knows what things you have need of even before you ask" (Matthew 6:8). There is no need to tell God about your problems. There's no need to beg and plead and supplicate help. I jokingly say there's no point in asking God to do something for you because God has already done everything that he can *ever* do, period. We are without end because God created you in the beginning in his image and likeness.

## Consciousness Is the Key to Prayer

Now you may say, "Where does God come in, then?" Well, God doesn't come in. God never went out. God is Spirit, present in its entirety at every point in space at the same time. God is the answer, and God is present so the answer is present. Whatever it is that you're seeking to understand, whatever guidance you need, whatever thing that you feel needs to be expressed or experienced in your life, it is present, total, complete, or it doesn't exist at all. There is no point in asking for something that is outside of your present awareness and your present relationship in the divine flow.

We need to get into the consciousness of oneness with God. It's not a matter of trying to get God into us, but of you and I getting into the awareness of that which is present. Consciousness is the key. We live in Divine Mind. It is impossible to have a mind apart from Divine Mind. You don't have a mind that is separate and apart from the Infinite, and if you think so, that is an illusion. Your mind is an activity within Divine Mind, a state of consciousness of Divine Mind. Life can only be understood when we know that we are always in fluctuating states of consciousness. The key to healing and overcoming is changing consciousness. This is what prayer is all about.

## PRAYER AS THE SCIENCE OF BEING, NOT DOING

Prayer is not something you learn to do, like learning to drive a car, learning to type, or even working crossword puzzles. A little girl was once asked when company was present to come out and say her prayers for the company, because her parents were delighted with the way she could say her "Now I lay me down to sleep." The little girl came out, all agog with the anticipation of performing before the guests, and she stood there, closed her eyes, and said her little prayer. They were all very flattered, and they praised her and they loved her and blessed her, and the little girl finally blurted out, "But you ought to hear me gargle!"

This prayer technique was something she had learned to do, some words she had learned to memorize, a pose that she had learned to take on. We laugh at this, and yet to a large extent this is the way prayer is involved in by so many praying people. It's something we learn. We go to catechism school, we learn to get involved in the experience by learning the words and taking on the pose, learning when to stand and when to sit and when to kneel and when to speak. Yet prayer is not simply a scientific way to do something; it is the very science of being. This is an important distinction. Otherwise, the emphasis is placed purely on performing the ritual, speaking the words, going through the outward experience of that which we've learned to do.

## Prayer as Consciousness of the Allness of Life

The key to understanding prayer is Allness. I use this term often, but it's so important. I use it interchangeably with the word *God*. So often when we use the word *God*, we think out, we think up, we think something separate. As long as we think something separate, we've created a separation that exists only within us, and otherwise does not exist. Prayer can only be effective when we think oneness. So instead of thinking of God, I think *Allness*. Allness means totality. It's not out there somewhere, it's the whole thing. In other words, you might use the word *universe*, the whole of things. All life is present. If there's Allness, the whole is present, all life is present, all wisdom is present, all substance is present, all guidance is present, all love is present. We live and move and have our being in this Allness, which is present, not absent.

Prayer is not trying to get more life, to get more love from God, but instead to know our oneness. The psalmist sang, "Be still and know that I am God." Trying to get more is to be still and know that I am, that I am the activity of life, all life, expressing at the point where I am. I need to know that. The fact is, we don't know it, and because we don't know it, we lose the consciousness of it. When we're out of the awareness of the Allness of life, we experience separation and deterioration. The need is not for God to give us more life, but for us to be more aware of the Allness of life, which is present in how I live and move and have my being.

The wonderful part of the creative process is that the Allness is ever seeking to fulfill itself in the eachness. This is a play on words, but it's important that we see this. I am an eachness within the Allness of God.

Jesus would say, "It is the Father's good pleasure to give you the kingdom," and the kingdom, he says, is not here nor there, but it's within you. The kingdom is the whole that is present even in the part. The kingdom is the oak tree that is present even in the seed. It's the Christ that is present even in the disbelieving person. It's the Allness of God that is present in the individual at the point where he is.

## GOD IS PRAYING FOR YOU

What this says, in its simplest possible terms, is that while you may be involved in praying to God, the ultimate reality is, God is praying for you. As Jesus told us, "It is the Father's good pleasure to give you the kingdom." The Allness has but one intent as far as you're concerned: to perfect itself and to express itself in and as you. Life is seeking to fulfill itself in you, in the renewing process of your body. Love is constantly renewing itself in you.

The Bible says, "For I have loved thee with an everlasting love" (Jeremiah 31:3). Guidance is a principle that is ever-present, always seeking to direct you and guide you at the point of your experience, in every turning of life's way. Allness is always seeking to express itself in the eachness, so that God is always praying for you. This is why I so often say, "Don't pray to God, but pray from the consciousness of God." First of all, be still and know that I AM. You don't have to reach a transcendent God, you have to reach yourself. You have to wake up. Stop thinking in terms of separation and absence and saying prayers and doing all sorts of magical things that you think are going to cause something out here to come into you. Be still and know my oneness. Be still and know that I AM, that God is present, not absent. Knowing that, I become relaxed and receptive. I allow the infinite process to simply do its perfect work, and its perfect work is to express itself totally and completely in me. It has no other intent as far as I'm concerned, except to hear me, to guide me, to direct me.

## Claim and You Shall Receive

Why would Jesus, then, indicate that we should ask God for help if we want answers? "All things you pray and desire and ask for, you shall receive," he said (Mark 11:24). This little word, *ask*, has created a lot of confusion. Quite often people say, "I ask God for this or that, and God just says no." The implication is that God doesn't like me, or that God's too busy about other things, or perhaps that he wants me to suffer for some inscrutable reason of his own, and of course a lot of religious tradition has rationalized man's problems in this way.

But Jesus says, "You ask and you receive not because you ask amiss" (James 4:3). You ask in a begging attitude, you're pleading and supplicating for something, something that is already the reality of your being. If you look up the word *ask* in the Hebrew Bible, the Latin, or the Greek, the root words as they are translated from the scriptures, you find that the strongest connotation is to *claim* or *demand*. Not to beg, but to claim. You ask for electricity when you walk into a room by claiming it, by turning on the switch. The power is already there, but you claim it. The Old Testament says, "Concerning the work of my hands, command ye me" (Isaiah 45:11). Now this is a vital realization of Truth. You ask for light by getting out into the sun, or by raising the shades. You ask for air by opening the window. You ask for health and for life by accepting it, by claiming it, by demanding it. You don't have to beg God to hear you because God, as far as you're concerned, is the healing principle that is ever-present. God is the perfect life and health within you.

Sickness is not the result of something God has done to separate Himself from you, but like the Prodigal Son, we have gone out into the far country and have separated ourselves from God and life. The need is not to get God to heal us, but to accept the healing life that God is and which is present and can never be absent, except that we think it is absent in our own consciousness.

# HOW TO ASK FOR HELP

This little word *ask* is a great problem. A creative way of asking for help is to create the condition that makes the result inevitable. You "ask" for electricity by throwing the switch. You throw the switch, you make a contact, and when you make the contact, this results in a flow of electrical energy into the circuit and into a filament of the light, which thus gets warm and heats up and becomes white and becomes the light of the room. You make it inevitable simply by making the contact. This is how it is in all things. You create the conditions that make the result inevitable. You create the condition in consciousness that makes healing inevitable when you synchronize your thought and lift yourself to a high level of consciousness in which you believe you are a spiritual being, one with divine life. You accept God's healing life, not begging, not supplicating, but you accept it. You claim it, you demand it. Synchronized in consciousness, the result of the healing flow is inevitable. It's not something that God does specially for you because he likes you or because you pushed the right button. It happens because you have allowed to be that which is, but you've allowed it to be for you, because you get into our consciousness of being.

Problems in our experience come because of our negative or "no" awareness. We ask for divine help by getting to a positive or "yes" consciousness. That's why we say all the time, "You can change your life by altering your thoughts." When you alter your thoughts, you don't change God's will toward you, because God's will toward you is fixed and final. It can never be anything else, except the infinite desire to perfect himself in that which he has created—to be health, to be guidance, to be life, to be love, to be substance in you and for you and through you. But if you change your thoughts, and thus you get into a "yes" consciousness, you become synchronized with the divine flow, and you create the condition that makes the result inevitable. It's important we understand this, otherwise we think of positive thinking as a little exercise in hypnosis or autosuggestion and so forth. *It's not this at all.* True positive thinking is simply synchronizing yourself with the great positive, with the great yes of Spirit, and thus you create the condition that makes the result of health and healing and guidance inevitable.

## LIFE-NEGATING CONSCIOUSNESS

We tend to spend so much of our time, of our waking moments, in a life-negating consciousness. If we could just become aware of how negative we are much of the time, we'd see how we are creating our negative conditions.

In the name of "being realistic," we spend our time in a life-negating consciousness, when our great need is to turn to a life-affirming consciousness. "Be ye transformed by the renewing of your mind" (Romans 12:2). This is what prayer is. It's not dealing with some special appeal to the heavens, but it's a systematic, scientific way of changing your thoughts and getting yourself in tune with the divine flow. The important thing to understand is that there is no way that God can answer your prayer without something happening to change your consciousness. If we want to carry that to the extreme, we can also say there is no way that

God can change your consciousness. The traditional understanding of "God" finds this incomprehensible.

God is the ceaseless longing to express totally and completely in you, but as long as you have a negative consciousness, you have the "on" switch turned off. You're separated, you're frustrating divine flow, and you're not allowing it in absolutely any way to flow through you. God can only do for you what he can do through you. That's a statement I have turned into a Butterworth cliché. *God can only do for you what he can do through you.* There is no way God can answer your prayers except by the change of your consciousness, and God cannot change your consciousness—only you can.

This puts the burden right back on our shoulders. So often we tend to deal with God much as people deal with a doctor. People overeat and overindulge and behave unwisely, and then they go to the doctor and expect the doctor to heal them. Quite often the doctor may be very gracious and may be thinking more in terms of her practice, and she may not say, "Look, you better stop indulging yourself or else there's nothing I can do to help you." The doctor will often give you pills and pat you on the hand and say, "You'll be all right, just take this three times a day." It is unlikely that a doctor can help you. If you're doing something wrong, you have to stop doing it.

Like I said, it puts the burden right on us. I know a lot of people tell me that I'm really hard on them. Maybe they'd like me to just give them a lot of soothing potions and tell them, "Everything will be all right, dear. It's fine. Just go out and know that the world is in divine order, people are great, and you're great and wonderful. Just keep doing as you are, only just accept that it's a wonderful life."

Perhaps some of us would like that. Maybe we would become suckers for that kind of approach. But I want to be very frank here: There is no way that you can change your life without being involved in the changing process. You have to do it. If you want to stop taking on the kinds of calories that make for obesity, you're going to have to discipline yourself to cut down on the calories. Nothing can do it for you, you can't find any magic diet, you can't find any great nutritionist, and not even God can help unless you exercise the will to push yourself away from the table.

## GETTING TO A 'YES' CONSCIOUSNESS

This happens in prayer. It comes right back on your consciousness, to your thoughts, and your need to discipline yourself. The marvelous part is the responsibility is on you, but so is the privilege. You have the Allness of the infinite process of God ever with you, and it is His good pleasure to give you the kingdom. It's all present; all you have to do is throw the switch. It's not easy because most of us have covered that switch with all sorts of negativity. We can't even find it, let alone throw it.

All we have to do is say *yes*. That's what true scientific prayer is. It's getting into the "yes" consciousness. God always says *yes*. We have to say *yes* to God's *yes*. What often happens, in the study of metaphysics, is we get too involved in affirmations and treatments, and while this is a helpful way to get into the flow of a spiritual awareness, sometimes we spend so much time trying to treat a problem. We get the *problem* at the center of our consciousness. It's like when someone says, "I have no tension, I have no strain, I have no resistance in me at all." He says this over and over again, and what he's really saying is that tension and strain and resistance are his problems. Emmet Fox would say, "Don't think about the problem. Think about God."

Basically, the need in prayer is to let go. Let go, and let God. Know that God knows, and God is always saying *yes*, and you say *yes* to God. Get into a "yes" consciousness, and you create the condition that makes the result inevitable.

## Prayer as an Affirmation of the Truth

This is why a prayer should be an affirmation and not a supplication. It's crucial we understand that affirming the Truth does not make it true. What you're really doing is creating the conditions in your consciousness, getting yourself on the "yes" level, and lifting your awareness to the divine level while synchronizing yourself to the divine activity. You are creating the condition that makes the result inevitable, but you're not moving God by your prayers. Otherwise, you're like the little girl who wanted us to hear her gargle. You don't get points for how well you say your affirmations. You may know the most affirmations and treatments in the world. You may have so many that you feel that this is really the result of your years of study. I've often facetiously commented on the fact that many Truth students exchange affirmations like little kids exchange baseball cards. "Here, I'll give you three Ralph Kiners for one Babe Ruth." "I'll give you this affirmation for arthritis if you'll give me one for heart trouble."

We tend to think that the word itself is some magic formula. "Oh, I got a great affirmation. I got a great treatment. Oh, this is marvelous." I don't want to disabuse you of something that may be very dear to you, but let's shock you anyway. There's no power in the affirmation. The power is that which can flow through the light switch if the light switch creates the condition that makes the result inevitable. The affirmation or the treatment is not the power, but it can, if used properly, lift your consciousness to awareness where the power may flow through. When it does, as Jesus said, "The words I say are not my words, but the words of him who sent me."

True prayer is not just a set of metaphysical truisms. It is not just substituting words of Truth for the ritual ones out of the prayer book. The power is not in the words at all, but in the life-affirming attitude. This life-affirming attitude is so important, so real, so true, that if you get that consciousness, you really don't even need the words. True prayer is not in words at all. The words may help us get into a consciousness of prayer, but you can pray without any words.

Words simply say *yes*, or should do so, to the transcendence of life. Jesus warns, "Use not vain repetitions, but enter into the inner chamber and close the door" (Matthew 6:6-7). Certainly, a lot of traditional religions need to know that, but a lot of people in metaphysical studies need to know it too. When was the last time you used a prayer affirmation over and over because you read that it's what you should do? Jesus says, "Use not vain repetitions." You're not going to be heard because of how many times you speak the prayer. Instead, enter into the inner chamber and close the door. Enter that inner consciousness of wordless silence. The Chinese have an ancient saying, "If a man be absolutely quiet, then the heavenly heart will manifest itself." That's not easy! Silence is difficult for most of us. You see, in this quiet or Silence there is no pressure to achieve anything. There is nowhere to go. It's not running from self to find some transcendent vision of reality. It is letting go of the masks of human consciousness, to know oneself at the point of God expressing as you.

## AFFIRMATIONS BEGIN WITH STILLNESS AND THEN LISTENING

You see, this first step of the Silence is what I often call the missing link in metaphysical treatment, or the affirmation process in Truth. We have a tendency to start frantically voicing affirmations with emphasis upon their repetition, upon the tone of voice, and on the fervency of emotion. But all of this is our version of "You ought to hear me gargle."

Often missing is the first step, "Be still, and know that I AM" (Psalm 46:10). In that knowingness, in that stillness, listen. You're a whole creature. In all experiences, something within you is seeking, even if sometimes unsuccessfully, to communicate itself to you. Even a headache is trying to say something to you if you'll listen. It's your body saying, "I need attention, I need help." Quite often we don't listen, and we pop an aspirin in our mouth. We pay no attention, really, to what it's saying at all. Every problem—relationship problem, financial difficulty, physical problem—is life trying to communicate something to you. If all we do is start mouthing affirmations, we miss the beat. Instead, repeat: "Be still, and know that I AM." Be still, be still, be still, be still, and listen. Listen and realize what you're listening to.

I feel that a person never gets the full message of Truth or going beyond the naïve approach in metaphysics until he begins to let go of the tendency to use stereotyped affirmations and treatments. It's like a child using training wheels on his bicycle. They help the child to ride for a while, but we would think it very foolish if a child would spend the rest of his or her life riding a bicycle with training wheels. If you saw someone riding around Central Park on Sunday afternoon with training wheels on his bicycle, you'd say, "Hey, he never grew up."

You know riding a bicycle requires a certain amount of balance, and it certainly requires discipline and training. Repeating an affirmation is a training process, but ultimately we need to evolve the tendency to use the affirmations that come out of our own self, spontaneously. Don't say, "I can't do that because I'm not very articulate," because that's to put yourself down, out of our Silence. Listen and then say what you're listening to, and if what you're listening to is Silence, then give an articulation of Silence. Sometimes it's better not to speak a word than to speak a word perfunctorily or automatically or hypnotically. Listen, and then say what you're listening to. The principle is to listen—be still and listen. In that point of Silence, something dynamic is at work within you, and you experience it, and you project it.

A student of Truth quite often mouths affirmations as if he were throwing darts at a board. He has a problem out there, and he beats it over the head with a cosmic club. He throws affirmations and barbs and arrows constantly. "You're God's child, you're wonderful, you're in tune with the infinite." Bang, bang, bang. He's throwing these things out. Watch an archer. He doesn't try to fling his arrows at the target. He stands at the line, and he fixes the arrow to his bow. He draws the bow back, building up an energy force, and then he doesn't push the arrow back. He simply releases it. The arrow goes straight and true, but not because of his will. "Not by might nor by power but by my spirit, says the Lord of hosts" (Zechariah 4:6).

The affirmation is not something that you express with power. I've heard teachers often say, "Speak the word with power so that God will heal." Well, God's not deaf, and Infinite God knows you better than you know yourself. His is the very word you're speaking. It is the power that you're using. So you're kidding yourself. The important thing is, be still and listen, and articulate the word, even if it's a word that you've taken out of the book. That's all right. Speak it, not as if the word is going to do some great thing. Speak it as if you're in tune with the power that does the great thing. You simply whisper the word, and you let it go, and the word goes forth.

Again, as Jesus would say, "The word is not my word, but the word of him who sends me." Now this is so very important. It's something we need to work on in consciousness to fully realize it.

## THE SILENCE

When I use the word *Silence,* I'm referring to what is often called meditation. I prefer the term *Silence* because it is still pure. *Meditation*, as a word, has been so influenced with all kinds of notions and philosophies and techniques as to almost lose its validity.

I always like to quote the great yoga master Aurobindo, who says, "It's not necessary to tell anyone how to meditate. If he is sincere enough, and open enough, he will find a way." Sometimes the meditation that is entered into in a technical sense, using the correct procedure, stops short of a spiritual process. It becomes a helpful therapy for relaxation and overcoming stress, and this is fine. But it does not become a part of the process of spiritual prayer. True meditation, or as I am terming it, the Silence, is not going somewhere. It's not reaching something, it's not even reaching for something. It's giving up the very desire to reach. This requires a great change in consciousness because most of us are doers. I want to get it done. I want to meditate. I want to use the right technique. I want to get there. We have a tendency to use the unconscious to try to reach up and into the very levels of consciousness, up there somewhere.

But when you do this, you haven't gotten any closer to spiritual reality than you were in the beginning. This is because God isn't up there on top of the mountain. God is the depth within you. Enter into the inner chamber, and close the door. The presence of God is not something to get into, or something that you can fall out of. The presence is present here and now. Any attempt to find or to reach the presence is to practice the absence of God. You want to practice the presence, not the absence. If you're talking to God, reaching for God, meditating to get into a higher consciousness up there somewhere, you're practicing the absence of God. You need to practice the presence of God.

# PRAYER AS CONCENTRATION FROM THE CENTER

I like to make a distinction between meditation, or the Silence if you prefer, and prayer. Meditation is concentration at the center, while prayer is the concentration of thought from the center. Now get this quite clear. One is to center yourself at the point within you, which is God expressing himself as you—not doing anything—just knowing it. This is meditation, this is the Silence. This is inner prayer. What we call prayer, the affirmation, the treatment, as a projection of this consciousness, is something else, very important and very real. In one case, we get centered, we know our oneness, we get the feeling of wholeness and Allness at the center. We get this feeling that Plotinus expresses when he says, "The whole universe rushes, streams, and pours into me from all sides while I just sit quiet."

Just know that prayer, as we normally think of it, is the projection of this consciousness.

So then, out of this awareness, I look upon the thing that I'm concerned about, not with my eyes opened, but I look, I center my attention upon it, and I see the light of this inner power flowing forth. I don't make it go forth, but I see it going forth, just like turning a spotlight upon something, coming out of that centered awareness. But the important thing is that we always need to begin with this consciousness of inner centering. I said this is the missing link in most metaphysical prayer treatment because most of us think of prayer and treatment simply as a matter of knowing and expressing a lot of words. Always, the first step should be, "Be still, and know that I am God."

## PRACTICAL ADVICE ABOUT WHAT TO DO IN PRAYER

Forget about the problem for a moment. If you want to, if you want to have a prayer time, write on a piece of paper the concerns you want to address, the persons, the situations, the job relationship or the problem with your boss, difficulties in the office—write it down so you'll be aware of it. You can write any affirmative thoughts that you'll want to use relative to that, if you care to do so. Lay it aside, and with that totally out of your mind, just be still. Enter into a consciousness of inner centering as if you didn't have a care in the world.

That takes practice. Just go down into the wall of inner consciousness, and center yourself. Get the feeling that the universe is already working through you, and remember, you don't have to pray to God—God is praying for you. Be still and listen. Just be relaxed, be receptive. People say, "Well, what do I do? What do I say?" Don't do or say anything. True silence or prayer is not doing. It's the exact opposite, and that's why it takes discipline. Just be still and let go. Listen. Get the feeling that the whole universe is pouring into you tremendous power, love, substance, intelligences. Pouring into you like the charge going into a battery while the battery just sits. The battery doesn't have consciousness, so it doesn't resist. It doesn't say, "Hey, I've got to start these cars." It just accepts.

Think of yourself as a battery, accepting, receiving, storing up as the infilling process of Spirit flows into you as you center yourself at the point of consciousness. Don't think of drain, restrain, or emptiness. Think only of wholeness and fullness. How long? There's no time in Spirit. Fifteen seconds? Two minutes?

Ten minutes? Not too long, because our consciousness begins to stray. Actually, a matter of a few minutes is about all you need. But always let that be the starting point for all kinds of prayer. Treatment, affirmation, anything, always take time to create the condition that makes the result inevitable, to get the light switch turned on, to remember that it is not my power but the power of Spirit flowing through me. Make contact with the power. This is the archer, pulling back the arrow, building up the energy, so that when you get ready to speak the word of Truth, affirm the Truth, or whatever your prayer process may be, you won't have to fling the arrow. You simply release it.

You don't have to dynamically project this affirmation or treatment, but you simply whisper it, you voice it. Silently, quietly, that power is that which flows through the affirmation and uses it purely as a vehicle, as a conduit. It goes forth to accomplish that work to where it is sent.

## NEVER PRAY WITHOUT ESTABLISHING ONENESS

Never pray until you've taken this time of oneness. This is the power, this inner awareness. Simply by letting go of the problem, and knowing oneness, the concern about the problem and the problem itself disappears into nothingness. In most cases, when we really understand the spiritual process, we enter into silence, wordless silence. When we're still enough, as the Chinese say, "The heavenly heart reveals itself." When we're still enough, suddenly we feel a flooding within us of a light process, a transforming healing process, and we find ourselves thinking, "Amen. It's all over." Then you look around and say, "I can't even remember what it was I was going to pray about." That's true answered prayer because it's dissolved, it's done, it's finished.

Most of us are verbal creatures, and we may want to verbalize it through an affirmation. Okay, fine, but be very sure that your affirmation is not an attempt to make it happen. If you try to make it happen, you're in human consciousness, you're in willfulness, you're in the ego, and you're also practicing separation. Just be still and know oneness, wholeness. And let it happen.

## MEDITATION—FEEL GRATITUDE

*Let's take a moment to be still. In this stillness I want to suggest feeling a sense of gratitude. That's all, just feel grateful. If there's ever been a time in your life when you've had a tremendous sense of gratitude for something that's happened, you can probably remember that exhilarating feeling. Let your consciousness now express and experience that exhilaration. Just feel it.*

*This is also to create the condition that makes the result inevitable. This is why we give thanks. We don't give thanks to God because God needs it, because God is an Allness too great, too universal to require our thankfulness and gratitude and praise and appreciation. We don't give thanks to God for his sake, but for our sakes, because the gratefulness gets us into a full-of-greatness consciousness. As we feel grateful, we throw the switch, and we create the condition that makes the result of dynamic life and the flow of intelligence and love and peace and power come through us and manifest as us effectively.*

*May you nod at this consciousness of gratitude, of thankfulness and praise, and experience that infinite flow. May it feel so good that in the days to come you will practice this many times over, and experience this same flow as you throw the switch in a feeling of gratitude. Praise God for the Truth that makes us free.*

# 8

---

# DEMONSTRATION

## YOU SHALL KNOW THE TRUTH AND THE TRUTH SHALL MAKE YOU FREE

YOU SHALL KNOW the truth and the truth shall make you free. This is a fundamental concept in the teachings of Jesus. It is a basic premise in what we have been calling *practical metaphysics*. This is a key to scientific prayer. What you experience will always depend on where you are in thought, in consciousness, in feeling, in self-awareness. This is so fundamental that if the focus of your thought is negative, the experience will tend toward limitation. This is something we study, we listen to, we practice to find wonderful realization. If your thought is centered in Truth, the tendency will lead toward wholeness in mind, body, and affairs. Now, obviously this is a great concentration of our whole teaching process, to try to get the focus of our attention in Truth.

In other words, you are *where* you are because of *what* you are. Now that's a very difficult teaching to accept, and lots of people don't want to accept it. You will recall it was said of Jesus that when he really got down to the nitty-gritty of his fundamental teachings, many people turned and followed him. It wasn't because they wanted to have pat potions, but because they wanted to have their hands held and their backs patted and so forth. But Jesus said, "I came not to send peace, but a sword." "I didn't come to love you into complacency, to tell you how lovely and wonderful and sweet everything is, but to help you to understand the Truth and know the Truth and find release through it."

So fundamental then is the fact that you are where you are because of what you are, because of what you are in consciousness, because of what you're thinking. If you're willing to take responsibility for your life, to really take responsibility for your thoughts and the patterns that go on in your subconscious mind, then even as your consciousness has put you where you are, so by a change of consciousness you can change where you are. You can change your experience. This is why I say you can change your life by altering your thoughts. It's that fundamental. It's the law that's always working whether we know it or not, whether we want to accept it or not. It's working even in times when it seems to be unfair.

## COMING INTO TRUTH BECAUSE OF A PROBLEM

It is probably true that most people have come to the experience of Truth simply because of some personal problem. Then this is somehow the way human consciousness tends to work. Most of us have come to understand the Truth or come at least into the "aura of Truth" at times when we're at our lowest ebb. This is a time when we've come to look for help and healing through this "Ye shall know the truth and the truth shall make ye free" process. Truth or New Thought or practical metaphysics is normally viewed as the science of problem-solving, and the chief teaching has become the secret of demonstration, which incidentally is a term most often used for answered prayer.

## THE PURPOSE OF TRUTH IS NOT JUST TO SOLVE PROBLEMS

I want to ask you something, because even though this is essentially correct, we need to see it all in perspective. Is the purpose of food to prevent starvation? Is the purpose of breathing to prevent asphyxiation? It might seem so—so it's in this context that we think of the purpose of Truth to solve problems. You need the Truth when you have problems, and when the problems are solved, then what? However, if we learn to eat and breathe correctly, then starvation and asphyxiation lose all relevance for us. They just don't exist in our life, they're not even possibilities. They become a part of the rhythm of life, and they're not last-ditch efforts to save us from difficulties. What we need to understand then is to receive the Truth not simply as a problem-solving series of techniques but as a fundamental key to abundant life.

We really begin to use the Truth. We are not simply using it to solve problems, but we come to the consciousness in which problems have lesser and lesser reality for us, and finally we don't even see problems as a part of our life. We know the Truth because it keeps us in tune with the dynamic upward swing of life. Jesus says, "Take no thought what ye shall eat and what ye shall drink, but seek first the kingdom of God and all these things shall be added" (Matthew 6:31, 33). He's saying take your mind off the idea of making demonstrations in life and begin to assemble your thoughts in the deeper awareness of life. Ultimately, you'll come to know that your demonstrations will make you. Truth begins to use us.

## THE SECRET OF DEMONSTRATION

We're talking about the secret demonstration today. You may think we're going to center all our thoughts upon how to make demonstrations, how to get jobs, how to heal yourself, or how to overcome your problems. Obviously, this is implicit within it all. But even as we're going to deal with the principles by which these things can happen, we want to be very sobering in helping you to understand that the whole idea of making demonstrations has been misrepresented and misapplied.

In an attempt to make the teachings practical, quite often teachers of Truth and books of Truth teachings have evolved extremely simple and sometimes simplistic techniques leading to demonstration. Now Paul says, "Be ye transformed by the renewing or your mind" (Romans 12:2). This is a dynamic realization, as there's no other way to be transformed, no other way to be changed, except to change your thoughts. To put this in its simplest possible way, and the way it has been presented normally in Truth, put a new thought in your mind to replace the limiting one. This is accomplished by suggestion, by affirmation, by treatment, by programming the mind with a new pattern, with a new attitude, with a new idea, a positive statement that articulates what you desire to be true and what you want to see manifest in your life. This is the way Truth is often presented: Just hold this thought in mind, and affirm it, and affirm it, and affirm it, or treat it and suggest it until it becomes established in mind. You will then demonstrate the help or healing you desire. It's as simple as that, or so it is said. It's a case of affirmations on the run for busy people.

## METAPHYSICAL HYPOCHONDRIACS

In the long run, even though a fundamental is correct, the approach can be completely oversimplified. It is a simplistic approach to the overcoming process, and thus is quite often extremely misleading. The result is we're basically involved, using the Truth to solve problems. I think many people in Truth become what I call "metaphysical hypochondriacs." They're not aware of this, but all they can see the Truth doing for their life is solving problems. They're always looking for problems to solve, and they never experience a transformative vision of themselves. So the person who is a good Truth student thinks of the practice of metaphysics as always trying to prevent starvation, to prevent asphyxiation. We never seem to get that thought as Jesus expresses, "Take no thought what ye shall eat, what ye shall drink" (Matthew 6:25). Take no thought that you've got problems moving before you. Instead, get yourself in tune with the dynamic spiritual process that takes care of itself, if you keep yourself in perfect peace, if you keep your mind centered in the light.

## NOT JUST MIND AND BODY, BUT SUPERCONSCIOUS SPIRIT

Consciousness work is fundamental. The subconscious mind will always tend to outpicture itself and this, too, is fundamental. But unless the patterns of the subconscious mind come from within, out of what we sometimes call the superconscious mind, and we're experiencing the pattern of our divine image and likeness, then what you're experiencing is what you had consciously put there through some treatment or another. It becomes the medicine you're taking, or the potions you're putting into your subconscious mind to try to reproduce themselves in your life. If so, we find that we have to continue to treat, over and over, just to maintain the conditions in our experience. We're constantly involved in saying, "Now, I've got to be very sure that I take this treatment, that I use this affirmation to correct that condition," but we do not along the way have the feeling and the faith in the superconscious process. We only see ourselves superficially and do not accept ourselves as whole creatures.

A great deal of the metaphysical system is taken out of context. I think the reason for this is our tendency to only think of ourselves as minds and bodies, and to eliminate Spirit. We need to shift our sense of identity. In our essence, a superconscious awareness is flowing through our subconscious mind. It is manifesting the image and likeness of the divine pattern within yourself. Otherwise, what happens is because we're not working from the foundation of our being, our wholeness in God. When we're merely treating a metaphysically affirming Truth, we unconsciously are trying to demonstrate wholeness as a condition "miraculously" formed from the outside, instead of awakening our unfolded activity of health from within.

Think of it in another sense: A person is in need of employment or he's concerned about his job, and so he seeks to demonstrate job security or to demonstrate a job itself. Imagine he has taken the whole process of his life out of the context of wholeness, and then tries to use Truth to "demonstrate" the job. He thinks of the job out there, the technique out there. Everything is out there trying to get it into his life, or to get patterns into his subconscious mind to reproduce them in his life. He doesn't seem to realize that the greatest need is to recognize his attunement with the divine creative flow. A job out there will always be a right and good job for you, or you'll be moved into a right and good place, if you're in tune with the idea of the creative flow within yourself. The demonstration of a job is not magically producing a job, but it's unfolding the consciousness that causes the job to come easily.

Unless we understand this, we may very well demonstrate the job, but the job has its own built-in limitations that tend to make the job unsuitable. Or the job runs out, so we have to demonstrate another one, and another one, and another one, always working to demonstrate, to bring health and healing and harmony and justice into our job and prosperity and success. But again we are engaged in the hypochondria process. The meaning is, as Jesus would put it, "Seek first the kingdom within" to the consciousness of your own divine flow. To demonstrate then, we seek awareness of the continuity of divine activity, and then all things will be added. The jobs will come, they'll come easily, but the demonstration is not materializing the job; it's spiritualizing your ideas about yourself in relationship to jobs.

This is subtle. A lot of folks have never quite grasped it.

If we're really going to make any progress in the demonstration of Truth, we've got to work from within out. The idea of demonstration is not working magic, it's not working miracles, it's not the *presto chango*, here it is, *ex nihilo*, something-out-of-nothing kind of process. It's releasing your imprisoned splendor. That which you desire is already within you, but there's something you have to do to release it so the demonstration deals with you, not with things that are happening to you.

## THE TEMPTATION OF JESUS

You may remember the wilderness story of Jesus, when he was tempted by the devil. Traditionally, we think of this Jesus, the great holy man, and the devil, this character with a forked tail and a pitchfork and fire coming out of his mouth, with the horns on his head, coming up to Jesus and tempting him. This is totally misleading. A much more useful way to see it is in terms of wholeness, so that the whole of each individual involved is the whole of you. From a symbolical point of view, the story of Jesus and the wilderness is the story of those experiences when we come face to face with our problems and with our own inner awareness of them. The saving that comes to Jesus is purely a part of his own subconscious mind; it represents the inner thoughts of his own consciousness, his own fears, his own inbred limitations.

We see Jesus in the wilderness, spending 40 days in meditation and reflection and coming to grips with himself. He finds the temptation of human consciousness seeking to lead him down the glorified path of individualized, miracle-working power, to use the ego-centered consciousness of power to do things. So Jesus gets hungry, and he had this great consciousness of power, so he was tempted to turn the stones into bread.

Then he was tempted to use his power for a worldly gain, to set himself on a throne. Why? Because he wanted to bring peace in the world and in the human consciousness. He felt perhaps, "If I could be the leader, I could set up a government that would do a little better, even as the politicians always feel the outs can be better than the ins. So I can do better than the Romans, I can do better than the Sanhedrin. I can run a government."

This is the human consciousness we all know so well, but Jesus came to grips with this, and by deeply knowing his oneness with the divine flow, he was able to say, "Get thee hence. Get thee behind me, Satan." He did not give in to the human of his consciousness that wanted to lead him down ways of self-limitation.

## CHRIST IN YOU, YOUR HOPE OF GLORY

One of the great secrets of the ages has by and large been lost under the weight of doctrinal confusion. It is found in Paul's letter to the Colossians, which is, "Christ in you, your hope of glory" (Colossians 1:27). This is a dynamic realization. Unfortunately, traditionalists have misunderstood and misapplied it and told us that Jesus is miraculously somehow centered in us. But we're not talking about Jesus. The key to Jesus' power, his demonstration power, the power to work so-called miracles, was the Christ in him, his hope of glory, his own awareness of the divine pattern established within him.

The secret of demonstration is the Christ in us, and what this means is to realize that the whole oak tree is established in the acorn. The secret of the demonstration of this growth process is the Christ in you, your hope of glory, the oak tree in you, your hope of the demonstration of the full process. It says that the Allness of the Infinite Mind is already enwrapped within you and always enwrapped within you. That's the means to unfold your good from within, and not simply to add it on from without. Let's be very sure that when we talk about the secret of demonstration, we're not talking about adding something on. We're talking about releasing your own uniqueness, which is the fulfilling of your own divine pattern, your own Christ in you, your hope of glory.

## God Can Only Do for You What He Can Do Through You

You are a limitless creature in Spirit, but you can manifest in your life only that much of the limitless that you can accept in your consciousness. *God can only do for you that which he can do through you.* This is something we've already explored. God doesn't work miracles for you, God *is* the great miracle that can be released through you if you expand your consciousness to accept it. But God doesn't work *for* you, God works *through* you—through your own participation. You don't have to get anything out of the universe. You've already been given everything because you are the universe or the Allness of God, a divine mind, expressing itself at the point where you are as you. The great key to demonstration is not to find something out there in the universe that will give it to you, but to become aware that within yourself you have the Allness of the universal flow. Allow it to demonstrate itself through you so then you're not really *trying* to make a demonstration, but to let the demonstration of life make you.

## THE TRUE DESIRE WITHIN YOU

The promise of practical metaphysics is that you can have anything you desire. That would seem to be a wild claim, like the claim of a politician who says, "I'm going to change all the world; just vote for me." You can have anything you want, anything you really desire. This is true because you cannot really, truly desire anything that is not already a part of the divine desire within you, seeking to express through you. Now the human of us has all sorts of feelings and sensations and the urge to acquire certain things as a result of our inquisitive instinct, our envies and covetousness. But *true desire* is that which is the Promethean urge within you. The Promethean urge is the upward pull of the Divine that is leading you toward that which is rightfully yours. You couldn't really desire it if it were not already yours. This is true if you see it from a perspective of wholeness, but there's different levels. When you see it in the level of Truth, it's one thing, but if you see it in the level of human consciousness, it's something entirely different.

Along the level of human consciousness, people often claim "anything I desire." I desire two wives. I desire $20 million.

I desire all the fun and all the activity that I want in my life, and none of the responsibility. You might think you desire all this, but if you're thinking in terms of human consciousness, separating yourself from the divine process, this is something different. On a divine level anything that you desire is the "desiring," the "siring" being the fundamental God consciousness here that is seeking to reproduce itself, the "de-siring" of this consciousness seeking to manifest itself in you, that which is yours already.

## DESIRE FROM HUMAN CONSCIOUSNESS VERSUS SPIRITUAL ONENESS

We need to see this rightly. If we see it only in part, then all we're really trying to do is fill our mind with covetousness, with the pictures of all the things we see in the world that we want to have in our own life, in our own experience. Too often we tend to do this by the technique of treasure mapping or visualizing or cutting the pictures of all the things in the magazine, and our mouth just waters. We imagine ourselves surrounded in full by riches, riches, riches, with gold as blessings coming down from the sky.

It seems like a beautiful thing, but it is not, because it deals with ourselves on a purely human consciousness. It deals with the most basic emotions of humankind, our selfishness, our inquisitiveness, our covetousness, our envies. While it is possible to demonstrate in this sense, we do not recommend it.

The important thing is to know that if we have a desire, if we go within, and listen to what the desire really is, it releases from within ourselves the unfolding process that eventuates in the kind of consciousness. If it's a car, for instance, that attracts the car, attracts the substance, attracts all the continuity of needs that may be a part of it, and it comes without effort. This is the outworking of "Seek the kingdom and all these things shall be added unto you." And this is the way demonstration should work when we deal with it in spiritual consciousness.

## THE MASTER FORMULA FOR DEMONSTRATION

There's a formula I have often used through the years. It's a formula I put together years ago, and it's become very popular. It's used a great deal through the whole metaphysical movement, and I'm very glad about this. It's what I call the Master Formula for Demonstration.

What it really says is C plus B equals A. This implies that what you can *Conceive* in mind and *Believe* to be a reality, you can *Achieve* or manifest. This seems simplistic, but it's simply a matter of trying to understand the process as it works. C plus B equals A. What you can conceive in mind and believe to be a reality, you can achieve or manifest in your life.

Again, the question is: What is it that you really desire? This is the starting point; it's where you are in consciousness. You have a physical problem, you need a job, you desire an increase in economic dollars and cents to help you to rise above the inflationary spiral, and so forth. This is where you are, and you can only start where you are.

# ROMANS 8:19—THE REVEALING OF THE SONS OF GOD

Paul has a statement that I love, "For the earnest expectation of the creation awaits the revealing of the sons of God" (Romans 8:19). Now your earnest expectation reveals your desire. Think about that desire, then the real fulfilling process depending upon the revealing of the sons of God, which means an awakening within you and your own divine pattern.

The secret of demonstration, then, is the releasing of that divine pattern within you instead of holding to the desire as a goal, holding it as a vessel you're determined to have filled: I have a physical problem, I have a relationship situation, I need a job, I need money, I need this, I need that. Instead of holding it out there to be filled, let it all go. Mind knows, the infinite consciousness within you knows, as Jesus said, the Father knows what's in your head even before you ask.

Before you ask, let it go. Lay it aside and turn within for a period of inner knowing. You don't even have to turn within and say, "God, I want to know what this desire means," because the activity of God and mind within you knows and knows that it knows. Just turn away from the desire and let go and relax and have a quiet meditation time and it will come to you. This is what Paul calls "the revealing," which is the *conceiving*.

This is the concept, the spiritual counterpart of that which your human consciousness is looking for—that spiritual counterpart is *always present*. If you have a physical problem, if you have a pain, you can know that humanly your desire is to overcome the pain, but then let it go, just relax, be still, and listen. There will come the divine counterpart that will reveal to you what the pain is really saying, what it's telling you, and you'll learn your lesson. And as you learn your lesson, the pain will disappear—instead of taking the aspirins and the pills or even the metaphysical "potions" to get rid of the pain and then still be left without a correction in consciousness for what the pain was really trying to lead you to in the first place.

## THE WILL TO DEMONSTRATE IS EGO-CENTERED

So human desire is all wrapped up in the ego and the world and will demonstrate as ego-centered. This is why we have a compulsion to talk about our demonstrations once we've made them. You ever wonder about that? It seems right, but remember Jesus says, "See thou tell no man" (Matthew 8:4). There was a reason for this "tell no man" consciousness, because if you want to tell everybody about it, you're relating to an ego fulfillment.

Demonstration comes easily. If you're constantly faced with a problem, if you have stomach ulcers after stomach ulcers, headache after headache, physical challenge after physical challenge, your body is trying to tell you something. If you have one rebuff after another in your relationships with people, then the fact is, something in life is trying to tell you something. The need is not to find someone that is going to take away your loneliness but to find what loneliness really means. Come to understand your relationship to the divine flow as one can never really be alone if he understands that he is already all one. When you get focus of divine flow, of love within yourself, then you find that the love process flows easily. You attract to yourself more relationships than you know what to do with, even the one relationship that becomes the fulfilling experience of love that everybody hungers for. But it comes easily not by grasping it. I often say, "In love, it's not a matter of finding the right person. It's becoming the right person." When you become the right person and understand yourself as a channel for love, you will always attract the right relationships easily and effortlessly.

It's the same way with a job, with money, and all things we try to demonstrate. Again, understanding that we're not trying to work out something from without, but we're trying to release that divine flow from within. If you pray for health and success, faith does not make you well or bring manna from heaven. It releases the divine flow that's already within you.

## THE BELIEVING POWER OF THE MIND

We see the second part of this C plus B equals A as the *believing power of the mind.* When you have this revealing—when you suddenly see and conceive of this idea, this identity, this inner need, and then believe it with the believing power of your mind—you will achieve. It's just as simple as that. However, we want to avoid this idea of the "magic" of believing, or we're right back into the mind alchemy syndrome again.

*Faith does not make God do special things for you.* As we've discovered, faith doesn't make things happen around you. Faith is the special state of awareness that accepts what God is and which in principle you have always been. It puts you in tune with divine flow and enables you to live with what Henry David Thoreau calls "a license of the higher order of beings." Things work easily for you because you're in tune with the consciousness of the divine flow. When you pray for health or success, your faith isn't going to make you well, your faith isn't going to magically bring manna from heaven. Your faith reveals the reality that is.

Faith is not a magic wand to making things happen; it is a perception that sees beyond darkness to light, a perception that sees beyond illness to Allness. It sees beyond the limited person to the Christ in you, your hope of glory, to the divine pattern.

## THE SPIRITUAL PROCESS IS AT WORK IN YOU ALL THE TIME

A spiritual process is at work in you all the time. When a person thinks in terms of the outward approach to Truth, it's like he's thinking about times when everything is arid, when there's no water, when we have a great drought as we see in nature. But in spiritual consciousness, there's no such thing as a drought. It's only a case of closing your eyes to the divine process, which is always present.

When you're in tune with God consciousness, when you really have the awareness that you are a spiritual being in tune with the divine flow, then no matter what difficulties are out there—a recession when unemployment is rampant, when your dollar is being eroded in terms of its value, even in the midst of this economic chaos—*it shall not come nigh onto thee.* That's the message in Psalm 91: "He that dwelleth in the secret place of the most high shall abide under the shadow of the almighty, it shall not touch you" (Psalm 91:1 KJV). There will be a self-regulating process that will make your money go further, which will work for you in spiritual economics. No matter what happens, it will not come nigh to you, according to the scriptural concept.

We're not trying to change things out here—we're trying to change the way we relate to them, the level of consciousness in which we function. By praying, you do not make God work for you, as we said in the previous chapter, but by praying, you evidence the fact that God is already working for you.

You pray, reflecting this God activity and allowing that God activity to express itself through you. Understand that, and condition yourself to get that realization in your consciousness, so that you will never again need to pray with a thought of, "Oh, God, help me." All the pleading and supplicating in the world is not going to cause God to be more than God or less than God. You cannot change God. God is the Allness that is present in your illness, the superconscious realization of Truth that is always present, even in your doubts and your fears.

## BE STILL—KNOW ONENESS—AFFIRM TRUTH

An affirmation is a very simple thing. It's simply the term that we use for scientific or metaphysical prayer. The old kind of prayer was intercession, asking God, interceding with God, trying to change God's will. The Truth approach is accepting the realization that as the scripture said, "Behold I have loved thee with an everlasting love." There is an eternal process, the Promethean will, that is always seeking to express itself through you. Before they call, I will answer, says the Old Testament. It is my Father's good pleasure to give you the kingdom, so there's something within you that's always seeking to express itself. We don't need to ask for help or to plead for help or to pray in a supplicatory tone but to add firmness. This is what the affirmation does. It adds firmness to our consciousness of oneness.

A treatment is a series of affirmations, Truth in which you evidence the fact that you're in tune with the divine flow. You're not making it happen, but you're waking up to the realization of the divine happening, which is always the reality of you.

## FAITH IS GIVING CONSENT TO THE CONSTANCY OF THE UNIVERSAL CREATIVE INTENTION

Faith is giving consent to the constancy of the universal creative intention, and this needs to be the "I am positive, I can" attitude. This releases the power and the skill that enables you to accomplish. When you believe you can do something, really believe that you can do it, then the how-to-do-it naturally unfolds. Think you can, and you'll unfold all the reasons why you can and how you can. Think you can't, and you will find 1,001 excuses why you shouldn't even try. That's the way the mind works. The potential is always present, but it's so easy to say, "I can't do it." If you say you can't do it, and deal with the things on the level of the "I can't consciousness," you won't do it.

There are valid reasons why you can't because you're dealing with it on the human level. But if I know that I can, and I can because I am a spiritual being, and the potential for achievement is always within me, always beyond my personal level of achievement, always beyond the past performance, always beyond what is on my resume, it doesn't make a difference what I've done. The potential for doing and being is always present in me because I am a spiritual being. If I deal with it on that level and think that I can, then the "how to" will easily unfold within my consciousness. This is the way Truth works, and we do use this time and time again, even if we don't know that we're praying.

## THE ACHIEVEMENT OF THE MASTER FORMULA

The "B" of the formula, the believing, simply means saying *yes* to the full implication of the "C," the ideal conception. Finally, the "A" of the formula, the achievement, would arrive instantly, *presto chango*, like magic. But this is not magic. When you conceive the inner vision to be for the greater good for you, then the next step is to be about your business and do what comes naturally, and it will come naturally.

You don't just sit with folded hands waiting for the good to manifest—get in tune with the divine flow. You do what comes naturally, and you will find it coming naturally for you to make the context, do the things, or as the Quakers would say, "move your feet." This is important because it is the activity of God in you that has revealed the goal, and which has given you the faith in the goal. It all comes out of the divine process.

## AFFIRMATION IS DEMONSTRATING FROM WITHIN

Now certainly it's important to pray and to affirm and to treat for results. Of course, this is a part of the divine process. But always remember that the affirmation and the treatment is not an attempt to make something true. Again, you can't make it true. If it isn't true, then forget the whole thing. If it is true, then it's true whether you know it or not, whether you use it or not, whether you demonstrate it or not. The affirmation is not to make it true, but to tune in upon the activity of Truth.

Quite often the hope for a demonstration becomes an end, a goal, a job, a healing, a relationship, an end that we're trying to achieve. A static condition of achievement or an object—something all wrapped up in a ribbon, something that allows the ego to say, "Look what I did, isn't it great? I'm really doing good these days"—but you see, even though we think of the goal as an end, life doesn't come to ends. This is why we have such great, puzzling feelings after we've had a demonstration, like the person who demonstrates a vacation trip. All the joy and anticipation of the trip is where the real feeling for it is. When the vacation trip comes to an end and it's finished, it's not nearly as fulfilling as it was in demonstrating it. This is in any aspect of life. Life doesn't come to ends; life is an experience in growth and going on. Many persons complain that they're not making demonstrations—they may be holding back their good because they're not *letting the demonstration make them.*

A person is praying for an increase in salary, a job, or better compensation, but if you're trying to demonstrate it with a pot of gold from the end of the rainbow, you're trying to do something outside of your consciousness. If you're working from within, you're seeking to demonstrate the kind of consciousness that's going to make this result inevitable. What does that mean? It probably means to work a little harder, go to work a little earlier, put a little more into your job—"move your feet," in other words. Get into the consciousness of creativity. Act as if you're already rich, act as if you already had all that you needed and felt good about it and you just went to work because you enjoy working.

Like a college professor said, "I would work for nothing, if I could afford it." He wasn't really being facetious, he was really saying that, "My work is not a place to make a living, but a place to make a life to live my making." It's so important to lift up our work into new consciousness, see it as an opportunity for you to project something of your own innate self. The need for greater supply or greater job security, you see, is that which comes not by making something happen out there, not by making a demonstration, but by letting the demonstration make me. For example: *I would be the demonstration. I will be the demonstration of the unfoldment of the creative process, which will enable me to put new enthusiasm in my work, give new ideas, think of myself as a creative channel, so that I know that it's an exciting opportunity that I have every day that I go to work to be a part of this creative flow, and I will let the demonstration make me.*

Suddenly all things will be added. The good job security, the money, and all the other good things in life, they come easily and naturally. I didn't make them, but something within me made me, and thus these are the things that were added. These are the real fringe benefits.

## TRUTH DEMONSTRATES ITSELF

We talk of demonstrating the Truth, and I think this is a term that Truth students use often. I say, don't try to demonstrate the Truth, it's a waste of time. *Truth demonstrates itself.* If you try to demonstrate Truth, then you're trying to do something in the ego, something in personal willfulness.

*Truth demonstrates itself.* The deed is to know the Truth and identify with the Truth. Get into the consciousness of what the Truth really is in terms of your life, and it will demonstrate itself. We see the secret to demonstration is a very simple thing: Know yourself. Know the divine pattern that was within you. Emphasize it, affirm it, and see it as flowing forth from within you, and the Truth will demonstrate itself and the demonstrations will make you all that you desire to do and be.

You don't have to create the good life, and you shouldn't try. The meaning is to unfold the good life. There's no need to program your mind with the success pattern and against the grain of a lot of metaphysical teaching. Again, you need not program your mind. As a matter of fact, to attempt to program your mind in most cases means trying to put something into your mind, trying to make your subconscious mind accept the fact that even though you are a swan, you will always be an ugly duckling. The need is not to program my mind so that I fit in out here, but to know that I have been programmed from within, from the beginning of time as God's image and likeness.

First is to know that inner awareness—the Christ in me, the hope of glory—and know that programs the subconscious mind with the belief of what I really am, not what I'd like to be, but what I am. Then it will reproduce itself in my life. But it will be real, it won't be superficial, it won't be a paste-on thing. It'll be what I really am in expression. You don't need to tell God what to do for you, or even try to direct the divine activity. You need only to, as the great Meister Eckhart says, "Let God be God in you."

## THE GREAT SECRET OF DEMONSTRATION

Remember, the great secret of demonstration is "Christ in you, the hope of glory." Christ in you being your own divine pattern, your own divine nature. You were created in the image and likeness of God in the very beginning, and it's always been so and can never change, world without end. The secret is the divine resource that is always within you. Jesus calls it the kingdom of God, and it's always within you as your resource.

The need is not to try and make it happen, but to *let* it happen. Not to make the Truth work, but to let the Truth do its perfect work through you and through your life. It's an easiness, and that's what it's all about. That's the fundamental part of this whole study of Truth that I think we need to get into our consciousness. The Truth is not something by which we can make magic demonstrations and work the "magic of faith and miracles" in life and so forth—it's *let go*. Not let go as in an emptiness of mind, not let go and just be lethargic and indifferent, but let go in the dynamic realization of the Allness of God within me and the divine pattern within me. It's the desire to let that divine pattern express itself in my life, knowing it will express in ways beyond anything that my human ego could desire.

Let go of the desire for the Mercedes, as it were, and you simply get in tune with the divine flow within you, and God-Mind knows your needs. You may still get the Mercedes, but it will come easily and effortlessly and in a marvelous, outward demonstration of what is a further revealing.

## Meditation—Unfolding of the Divine Pattern Within You

*In the course of this study of the nature of "practical metaphysics," the important thing to know is that you don't leave anything behind you. If anything has excited you, then it is already within you, and you've been excited by it because something of the divine process has been "insighted" with you, and that insight is a remembrance of what has been yours from the very beginning of time.*

*Just say yes to it, just acknowledge it, say, "Beautiful, wonderful. I thank the Father. Yes, it's true." And go on your way just feeling grateful. Grateful that you've been able to perceive it, to sense it, to experience it. It is you that experienced it in consciousness and it is you who has the answer even before you call. Truly, this is purely and simply a matter of awakening within ourselves the divine pattern, and I want to do that for myself. I want to be a greater channel for the receptive expression of this fundamental creative process, and I want to see you as being a greater channel. Namaskar, which is the Hindu expression for, "The divinity within me salutes the divinity with you."*

*I see in you this divine flow manifesting this day in greater and greater ways, and from that consciousness in myself, I say "namaskar." I see in myself this flow of divine creative expression unfolding in beautiful and wonderful ways. Each and every one of us, all of us together, and each of us separately, going from this place today, committed, dedicated, and consecrated to a greater expression of the Truth. The goal of course is to keep on. In the keeping on, there will be great unfoldment of the consciousness of God as a dynamic presence and power at work in every experience of our lives, helping us to meet every challenge, every turning of life's way, from the highest possible perception. Remember, as Ralph Waldo Emerson says, "For what is prayer, but the contemplation of the facts of life from the highest point of view."*

*Praise God for the Truth that makes us free. Praise God for the consciousness that perceives the Truth as the very wealth of the kingdom that is within us. And we let that kingdom come and allow that Promethean will be done in earth as it is in heaven.*

# ABOUT THE AUTHOR

Eric Butterworth (1916–2003) was among the leading teachers in modern times on "practical mysticism." Butterworth is considered a legend and spiritual icon in the Unity spiritual movement. He was the author of 16 best-selling books on metaphysical spirituality, a gifted theologian, philosopher, and lecturer, and for more than 50 years a teacher of "practical Christianity," helping thousands of people to help themselves to a more abundant life by the study and application of Truth. He possessed a unique ability to render the most complex metaphysical teachings in simple sound bites of awareness. He mastered the art of the brief "essay-ette," of which he wrote thousands, and is often described as "the 20th-century Emerson."

Born in Winnipeg, Canada, in 1916, Butterworth attended Fresno State University and Capital University in Ohio, where he studied music. He began training for the ministry at Unity Village in Missouri during World War II. He left to join the Army and, as a lieutenant in the Medical Corps, trained medical personnel, and also served as chaplain and counselor. After the war, he returned to his ministerial studies and graduated from Unity Ministerial School. He was ordained a minister in 1948. Butterworth established three powerful Unity ministries. The first was in Pittsburgh. He then moved to Detroit, where his teaching resulted in the growth of the Detroit Unity Temple, the largest Unity church at that time, where more than 2,000 people attended his Sunday services each week. While in Detroit, he authored his first book, *Unity: A Quest for Truth*. In 1961 Butterworth began his ministry in New York City. He lectured every Sunday at Carnegie Hall, then Town Hall, and after 1976, Avery Fisher Hall, where the weekly attendance grew to several thousand.

Eric Butterworth made his transition peacefully on Thursday, April 17, 2003.

Printed in the U.S.A                                    B0124